A Homeowner's Guide to Home Repairs

WITH THE RIGHT TOOLS AND THE RIGHT KNOWLEDGE, you can tackle any home-repair project with confidence. Stanley® has the tools, and with this guide, you have all the knowledge you need to get started—right now.

These days, the idea of diving into small jobs around the house rather than hiring a professional has a lot of appeal. Not only will you save yourself some money (and maybe some time), but you'll also have the satisfaction of "doing it yourself" and acquiring some new skills along the way—whether it's patching a hole in the wall, fixing a light switch, or painting your bathroom.

Top-notch homebuilding skills aren't an absolute necessity for successful home repairs, but they definitely help. *Fine Homebuilding* magazine is written by homebuilding professionals—carpenters, plumbers, electricians, and other tradespeople—who know the best way to get the job done. In this special issue, we've collected the articles that offer the best tips and techniques on home repair, from replacing a broken tile and installing a toilet to hanging a door and sealing a window. All that's left for you to do is pick up your tools and get started.

—Editors of *Fine Homebuilding*

STANLEY

Home Repairs

Editor: Christina Glennon
Copy Editor: Diane Sinitsky
Design and layout: Stacy Wakefield-Forte
Photographer: All photos and illustrations by Taunton Press
    staff © The Taunton Press, Inc., except where noted.
Front cover bathroom tile installation by Jimmy Tiganella,
    Classic Tile, Watertown, Connecticut

The following names/manufacturers appearing in *Stanley® Home Repairs* are trademarks: 3M™; Abralon®; Beadex®; Benjamin Moore®; Black & Decker®; Briwax®; ClingCover™; Dow® Weathermate™; Durock®; Elmer's®; FatMax®; Festool®; Floetrol®; HardieBacker®; I-Beam 180™; InSinkErator®; Jam-Buster™; Johni-Ring®; Laticrete®; Minwax®; Mirka®; Norton®; Peel Away®; Penetrol®; Phenoseal®; Sharpie®; Sherwin-Williams® ProClassic®, Duration®, and Emerald™; Speed® Square; Stanley®; Trim-Loc®; UGL®; Vol-Con®; Wiffle®; XIM Peel Bond™; Zinsser® Cover-Stain®

FineHomebuilding

To contact us:
Fine Homebuilding
The Taunton Press, Inc.
63 South Main Street, PO Box 5506
Newtown, CT 06470-5506
Tel: 203-426-8171

Send an email: fh@taunton.com

Visit: www.finehomebuilding.com

To subscribe or place an order:
Visit www.finehomebuilding.com/fhorder
or call: 800-888-8286
9am-9pm ET Mon-Fri; 9am-5pm ET Sat

The Taunton guarantee:
If at any time you're not completely satisfied with *Fine Homebuilding,* you can cancel your subscription and receive a full and immediate refund of the entire subscription price. No questions asked.

The Taunton Press
Inspiration for hands-on living®

CONTENTS

STANLEY

PAINTING TECHNIQUES

CONTENTS

STANLEY®

PAINTING TECHNIQUES

Prepping Before You Paint

BY JIM LACEY For a lot of people, painting is dreadful. They complain that it's messy and fussy, and that they don't always get the results they hoped for. The truth is that most people end up with less-than-desirable results because they ignore the importance of proper preparation.

In the 20 years that I've been painting houses, I've learned how to size up quickly the results of poor prep work. The signs include paint peeling in sheets off doors and trim, mildew seeping through layers of paint, and bleeding spots on walls and ceilings—paint failures that easily could have been avoided.

At each job, I follow a basic routine that ensures a long-lasting, attractive paint job. I start by removing items from the room. Large items, such as couches, can be moved to the center of the space and covered with drop cloths. With a fresh canvas, I can begin the real prep work.

Jim Lacey is a professional painter in Bethel, Conn.

1 DROP THE ENTIRE ROOM. After the furniture is covered or removed, cover the floor with heavy-duty canvas drop cloths. Use 9-ft. by 12-ft. drop cloths near walls, 4-ft. by 5-ft. cloths under tools and paint, and a 12-ft. by 15-ft. cloth to cover a large area of flooring or furniture. Don't skimp on the drop cloths. Cheap products can allow paint to seep through, and plastic drop cloths can be slippery, especially on hardwood floors.

2 ORGANIZE AND STAGE ESSENTIAL TOOLS. Keep all commonly used tools close at hand. This helps the work to go smoothly. Place these tools on their own drop cloth in an easily accessible but out-of-the-way area. Large items, such as stepladders and vacuums, also should be kept close by.

3 LIGHT THE SPACE. Set up halogen lamps on a stand, and clamp circular incandescent lamps wherever possible. Set the lights in a position that eliminates shadows and works best with the natural light coming into the room. Adjust the lights as conditions change.

5 **WASH DOWN EVERYTHING.** One-quarter cup of trisodium phosphate (TSP) per 2 gallons of water will remove dirt, smudges, smoke residue, and most surface grime. Pay particular attention to high-touch areas such as door jambs and areas around light switches. Bleach and TSP work best on mildew stains. Use a light hand when washing; you don't want to soak the wall. Also, wear heavy-duty rubber gloves. Allow the walls and ceiling to dry completely before moving on.

4 **REMOVE WALL AND CEILING OBSTRUCTIONS.** Don't try to paint around easily removable elements such as window treatments, sconces, outlet covers, switch covers, thermostats, and recessed-light trim rings. Large fixtures, such as chandeliers, can be covered with plastic instead of being removed. The escutcheons can be unscrewed and lowered.

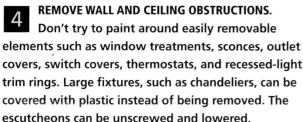

MUST-HAVE MATERIALS

- Stepladder
- Canvas drop cloths
- 5-in-1 tool
- Multibit screwdriver
- 2½-in. angled brush
- Acrylic caulk
- Cut bucket
- Extension cords

- Taping knives
- Paint trays
- Roller handle
- ⅜-in. roller sleeves
- Roller extension pole
- Bleach or TSP
- Rubber gloves
- Sponges

- Tinted primer
- Joint compound
- Tack cloths
- Sandpaper and sponges
- Rags
- Shop vacuum
- Auxiliary lighting

1 **ASSESS THE EXISTING PAINT.** Glossy finishes need to be sanded with 120-grit sandpaper, while moderate-gloss paint can be sanded with 120- to 150-grit sandpaper. Very hard surfaces may need to be prepped with a palm sander, but most often, you can get away with using a sanding sponge or sandpaper. Remove dust from the wall with a brush and a tack cloth.

2 **REPAIR ANY DAMAGE, AND FILL ANY GAPS.** Joint compound is ideal for repairing cracks, holes, or dents in both drywall and plaster walls. Use a high-quality wood filler for repairs on wood trim and doors. Sand the repairs, and remove dust from the wall with a tack cloth, a brush, and a vacuum. Any gaps that have developed between the trim and the wall or ceiling should be caulked. Acrylic caulk performs well in most applications. However, in damp areas such as bathrooms or kitchens, consider a vinyl adhesive-based caulk for greater longevity.

3 **MASK CONSERVATIVELY.** Mask only those horizontal areas that are most vulnerable to paint splatter, like the tops of chair rails and the tops of baseboards if they're not going to be repainted. If baseboards are going to be repainted, mask the area where the wood flooring meets the baseboard.

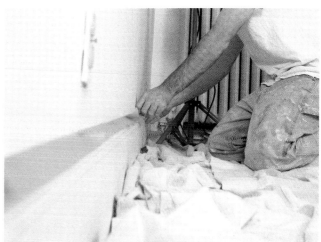

4 **ALWAYS PRIME WALLS BUT NOT CEILINGS.** Roll primer on walls to give paint a flat, uniform base to adhere to. Ceilings don't always have to be primed because they're often in good shape and are typically painted with flat paint. Recoating flat paint is less demanding than recoating glossy paint. You should, however, spot-prime areas with repairs, such as places that had water leaks or drywall cracks. Tinting the primer to the finish color helps to improve coverage and gives a better sense of how the room will look when it's done—much better than small paint swatches, which can bleed through subsequent coats of paint and ruin the final finish. Universal acrylic primers perform better than ever and have little odor.

5 **GIVE THE WALL A FINAL SANDING AND CLEANING.** Sand all wall and ceiling surfaces with a medium-grit sanding sponge, and inspect the surface for any irregularities, such as hardened paint or primer drips. This is an ideal time to make any final touch-ups or repairs prior to painting. If you make a repair, remove the dust, and be sure to spot-prime the area before starting to paint.

Cutting In Trim and Corners

BY JIM LACEY One of the benchmarks of a good paint job is crisp, straight transitions of color where trim meets a wall or a wall meets a ceiling. I've found that cutting in these areas is as much about having the right tools as it is about having the right technique. It all starts with the right brush.

My favorite is an angled sash brush. It's good for a wide variety of painting tasks besides cutting in. Most painters, pros and do-it-yourselfers alike, hate cleaning brushes; even some pros wrap their brushes in plastic wrap or aluminum foil for later use. Unless I'm in an extreme rush, though, I don't do it. Clean bristles produce a much better finish, and it really doesn't take long to clean a high-quality paintbrush.

Having a clean brush is so important that I wash my brushes both at lunchtime and at the end of the day. In hot or dry conditions, I may wash my brush three or four times a day. The problem with storing brushes in plastic wrap, foil, or even zip-top bags is that the paint near the top of the bristles dries in a few hours and becomes difficult to remove completely. Before long, the bristles don't hold as much paint or flex as they should, which contributes to a rough finish and ragged lines where you're cutting in.

Besides the brush, you need a paint pail. I like metal pails because they don't flex unnervingly like plastic pails; however, the seams in metal pails make them more difficult to clean. If you find this a problem, look for a paint store that sells liners for metal pails. I use them whenever I'm changing colors several times a day.

I fill the pail about one-quarter full so that there's plenty of room to tap off excess paint on the side. Generally, I find high-quality, well-mixed paint (I like Benjamin Moore®) to be fine right out of the can, but in extremely hot or dry conditions, a paint additive such as Floetrol® or Penetrol® (www.flood.com) can reduce brush marks and even the transitions between brushed and rolled areas. Follow the additive directions carefully to avoid problems.

Jim Lacey is a professional painter in Bethel, Conn.

5-QUART
STEEL PAINT
PAIL

5-QUART
PAINT PAIL
LINER

COOL TOOLS

Cutting in nice, straight lines starts with the right brush and a high-quality paint pail. A good paint-brush choice is an angled sash brush. Pails come in several sizes. Choose one that's comfortable to hold and has enough room for tapping excess paint off the brush.

3-IN. ANGLED
SASH BRUSH

1 WET THE BRISTLES. Before painting, wet the bristles in the appropriate solvent (check the can), and then squeeze out the excess. This makes cleanup easier and prevents paint from creeping up the bristles.

2 GET A GRIP. Hold the pail with four fingers on the bottom and your thumb wrapped around the handle. Keep only an inch or two of paint in the pail to keep your brush and workspace clean and to minimize spills.

CONTINUED ON PAGE 14 ▷

CONTINUED FROM PAGE 13

3 **TAKE A DIP.** Dunk the brush into the pail so that paint covers about one-third of the bristles. You can adjust the paint depth by tipping the pail slightly to the side.

4 **ONE TAP.** Tap one side of the brush against the side of the pail, and then gently drag the bristle tips over the rim. While painting, keep the pail in your left (or nondominant) hand for maximum productivity.

5 **APPLY THE PAINT.** Starting ½ in. to ¼ in. away from the trim or ceiling, use a single stroke to apply the paint. Looking slightly ahead of the bristles, pull the brush toward you; keep dragging until the paint stops covering.

6 **WORK IT OUT.** With the brush rotated 90°, take a second pass with the bristles just touching the trim or corner. The paint should level out, leaving a smooth line free of ridges. Take a third pass only when necessary.

Painting Trim the Right Way

BY TIM LEAHY   Most people who are new to painting see the job in terms of applying the finish coat, but that's just the icing on the cake. The real work that makes or breaks a paint job is how you prepare the surface. If you're painting interior trim and you don't do a good job of sanding, cleaning, and priming, the final coats of paint won't look pristine. At the very worst, a poor prep job can make the finish coats fail.

I work in high-end restoration, where the end result is paramount. Over the years, I have developed the following procedures for a great paint job.

Clear the Air

Whether it's your spouse, the construction manager, the homeowner, or any combination of the three, everyone needs to know when the painting stage of a job is set to begin. Other trades need to be out of the area, and the air needs to be right, especially for the last finish coats. The inside temperature should be between 55°F and 80°F, and the humidity level should be less than 50%. Humidity between 50% and 80% is less than ideal. When the humidity shoots over 85%, the paint won't dry properly, which may cause blushing, sags, wrinkling, or film failure.

Air quality is very important, especially during the finish-coat stage, so we try to eliminate all airborne dust by using fans fitted with filters to draw in clean air and exhaust dusty air from the work area.

FIRST THINGS FIRST. Before starting the prep, thoroughly vacuum the floor and all horizontal edges to eliminate dirt and dust. An aftermarket HEPA filter (inset) improves the performance of a typical job-site vac.

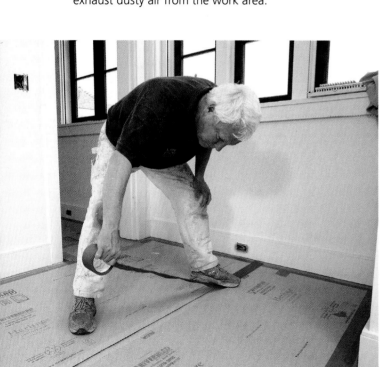

COVER THE FLOOR. It's a good idea to cover the floor with builder's paper to contain any embedded dirt. The author uses this quick method of footwork to apply tape to the paper.

Clean and Protect the Room

A dirty floor and fresh paint don't mix. The dirt gets airborne when kicked or when cords, hoses, or ladders are moved. Once everyone has left the area, the first thing we do is vacuum. Sawdust, dirt, and other debris on the floors and walls need to be cleaned off with a powerful vacuum that has nonmarring attachments. Vacuums equipped with high-efficiency particulate absorption (HEPA) filters are the best, although they can be expensive.

Any hardware should be removed or protected. We remove hardware, tag it with tape, label it with a marker, and place it into plastic bags or clean cups. If there is a lot of hardware, I use a camera or a sketch pad to document the layout before taking everything apart.

If the area has finished floors, we use one of three levels of protection. If we happen to be priming in a room where the flooring hasn't been finished, we tape down rosin paper, which helps keep the dust and dirt to a minimum. If the finish is in place, then we switch to a thicker, more protective paper product such as Ram Board, and sometimes even add a plastic layer to block moisture. The ultimate protection is paper first, followed by a layer of plastic and a layer of lauan plywood.

Fill the Holes

On many of our jobs, paint-grade trim comes to the site already primed. Once it has been installed (and if not primed, see "Apply the Primer" on p. 19), the next step is to fill the fastener holes. For typical finish-nail holes, I use lightweight spackle. I like UGL® brand, which dries quickly and expands out of the hole when dry, which makes it easy to sand flush with the surface. For large screw holes, I use a two-part wood filler. Lots of folks use auto-body filler, but I use a two-part filler from Minwax® that is made for wood.

For dents and shallow imperfections, I use Elmer's® Interior Wood Filler. This product has better adhesion than spackle, so it works on fine dents and scratches. It tends to shrink, though, so I have to compensate with a slight overfill or a second application.

FILL NAIL HOLES. Use a lightweight filler such as UGL spackling to fill small holes. Press the filler into the holes, and allow it to expand to prevent shrinkage.

LEVEL DENTS. Use a medium-body product such as Elmer's Wood Filler to fill any shallow depressions in the trim. Overfill slightly so that sanding will create a flush surface.

THINK BODY SHOP. For wide holes deeper than ¼ in., use a two-part acrylic product that is similar to auto-body fillers, such as Minwax's Wood Filler.

Sand Surfaces and Soften Edges

When the fillers have dried, it's time to sand everything smooth. This prep stage creates a uniform profile over the trim surface. Hand-sanding and checking your work by feel is critical; your fingertips can detect imperfections that your eyes would miss. I always use a disposable mask with a N100 rating when sanding.

I begin with 180-grit sandpaper to smooth the entire surface and to level all fills. Since fillers are often softer than the wood around them, I make sure to keep the paper flat so as not to dig out any filler. Working from the bottom up means not sanding over dust from above. I feel every inch as I go to ensure the surface is buttery smooth. At this point, it's OK to burn through the primer on some edges and profiles and to remove heavier raised grain. The primer used in the factory is typically applied heavily, which results in a poor texture that has to be sanded down quite a bit to create a truly flat surface.

Sharp edges are easily worn and chipped, so it's best to soften them with 150-grit paper. Remember, it's all about the feel. After everything has been sanded, I use a vacuum to thoroughly clean the surfaces, and then a raking light to inspect for defects. It's better to fill a spot now than it is to interrupt your workflow in the middle of painting to spackle a divot.

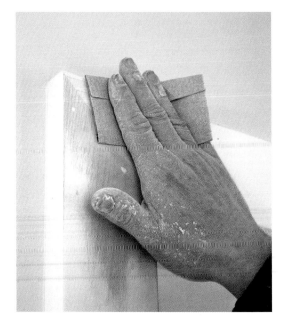

1 **PROPER TECHNIQUE. It's easier to control the work if you sand by hand. Fold the sheet into thirds, and hold it between your pinky and ring finger to keep it from sliding around.**

2 **DON'T FORGET THE EDGES. Make all surfaces consistent by sanding the edges of trim pieces and the adjoining wall areas.**

3 **SHINE A LIGHT. When a section is complete, use a strong light to make sure that all the imperfections are filled.**

4 **CLEAN UP. After sanding, be sure to vacuum the dust from the trim and the surrounding surfaces. Use soft attachments that won't ding the trim surfaces.**

Apply the Primer

We always make sure the trim has a total of two coats of primer. If you begin with unprimed trim, apply an oil-based primer to the entire surface. I like to use Zinsser® Cover-Stain® Primer because it seals off the grain and tannins better than water-based products, it sands smooth, and it can be topcoated with oil or latex. I have used water-based primers, but they tend to raise the grain, which means I have to prime and sand two or three times until the grain texture is tamed.

The second coat builds the surface, giving it an even color and texture that's a good substrate for any type of finish paint. Be sure to brush the primer onto the adjacent walls to create a better seal for the caulk. This foundation coat has to have straight brush strokes, minimal build, and no fat edges or overlaps. Brushing needs to be done in proper sequence: first the edges, then the flats.

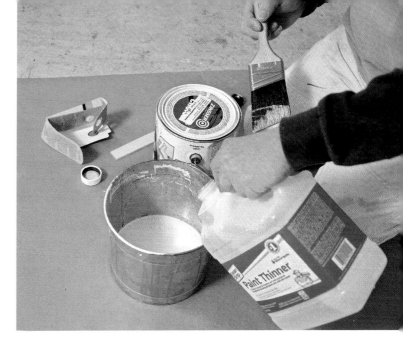

1 **THIN IS BETTER.** Many modern oil primers must be diluted with turpentine or paint thinner (about 1 part thinner to 10 parts paint) so that they soak into the wood.

2 **START FROM THE EDGE.** To avoid buildup, brush first from the edges of the trim, making sure to hit the seam between the trim and the wall.

3 **GET RID OF THE EXCESS.** It's difficult to brush away more paint than the brush can hold, so use a rag to wipe off the flats before proceeding.

Sand Both Primer Coats

I lightly sand the trim after both the first and the second coat of primer to remove dust nibs or unwanted texture. I also wipe down the adjacent walls and vacuum to remove dust before caulking.

1 **CREATE A GOOD FOUNDATION.** Working in one direction, brush out the face of the trim in even, straight strokes, being sure to avoid laps and drips.

2 **IT MAKES A DIFFERENCE.** After each coat of primer has dried, use 320- or 400-grit sandpaper or an extrafine nylon abrasive pad to prepare the surface.

PAINTBRUSHES

For even brushwork, you need a decent brush. Look for evenly cut, feathered ends on the bristles, which help to smooth out the paint.

Caulk Open Seams

For the last step before the finish paint, I fill all cracks and seams with a high-quality acrylic adhesive caulk. The main trick with caulk is to make sure that a good bead of it gets forced behind the surface of the crack. Joinery with gaps of less than 1/16 in. don't need to be filled as deeply, but anything larger should be filled behind the crack, not just on top of it. If the bead is too thin, the caulk will crack at the slightest movement of the underlying material. Once I've applied the bead, I use my finger to push the bead into the crack and smooth it out at the same time. I don't use rags, as they tend to wipe away too much caulk. Larger fills are prone to shrink and may need a second application.

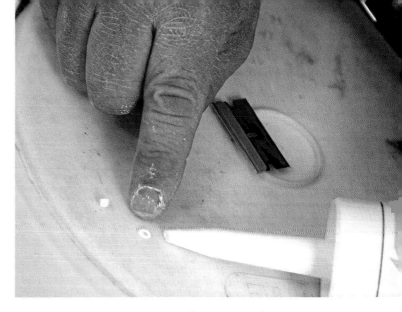

1 **CONTROL THE OUTPUT.** When you're about to use a new tube of caulk, cut off the tip at an angle so that the caulk can be easily directed into cracks without too much waste.

2 **PULL, DON'T PUSH.** With the angled tube facing the crack, pull the tube along the seam as you squeeze out a consistent amount of caulk.

3 **DIGITAL WORKFLOW.** Use a fingertip to smooth out the bead of caulk and to push it into the seam. Use a rag only to wipe off your finger, not the seam.

Apply the Topcoat

Vacuum as needed, then ensure that the air is as free of dust as possible and within the manufacturer's recommended temperature and humidity levels. Add heat to the room if it's too cold; if it's too hot and there's no air-conditioning, work at night. Allow for extra drying time if the humidity is high.

EPA regulations have adversely affected the performance of oil-based finish paints, especially in terms of their tendency to yellow over time. Fortunately, manufacturers have improved the performance of acrylic paints so that they level better and work easier than before. On this job, I used Benjamin Moore's Advance, which is a water-based paint with a small alkyd component to help it work and be tough like oil. Slight thinning according to the label directions is OK, but you shouldn't need any additives such as flowing agents.

Tim Leahy is a professional painter and restoration specialist with Kirby Perkins Construction of Newport, R.I.

1 **MIND YOUR STROKES. When applying primer or finish coats, keep the brush strokes definitive along transitions such as miters and other joints.**

2 **SCUFF AND BUFF. After the first finish coat has dried overnight, rub all areas lightly with an extrafine nylon pad or 400-grit sandpaper to smooth any imperfections and to dull the surface for the final coat. After vacuuming, wipe everything down with a tack cloth.**

3 **APPLY THE SECOND TOPCOAT. The final coat of paint should provide a perfect sheen and an extra layer of protection. After it has dried, check for missed spots and then clean the area, remove any masking, and reinstall the hardware.**

Skillful Brushwork for Doors and Windows

BY PHILIP HANSELL The paint protecting your doors and windows has a tough and important job to do. It must endure hostile weather, punishing wear, and up-close scrutiny every day. Paint made for doors and windows used to be judged by how much lead it contained—the more lead, the better. These coatings worked great. The heavy metal helped the paint to stick and to move seasonally. As is well known now, however, lead is toxic and is especially dangerous to kids. For this reason, lead has been banned from household paint since 1978.

Old doors and windows generally have high concentrations of lead paint, so it's important to protect yourself and any children who live in the house by working lead safe. This means containing and collecting dust and chips and minimizing airborne particles. Wear a good particle mask when scraping and sanding, and use a HEPA vacuum. Thoroughly clean up the work area every day, and change your clothes before playing with the kids.

Key Preparations

As with all painting projects, proper preparation is key for painting doors and windows. Before starting, my painters

and I wash the glass with glass cleaner and paper towels. We then mask the hardware and the perimeter of the glass panes.

Once the door is cleaned and masked, we fill any damaged areas with two-part auto-body filler and sand the dry filler with 180-grit paper. For the initial sanding on the rest of the door, we use 220-grit paper on the interior and 180-grit on the exterior. For the second sanding (between the first and second coats), we use 320-grit paper for interior work and 220-grit for exterior work. A rougher grit on the outside gives the surface a little more "tooth" for better paint adhesion.

All painting starts with prep

1 **MASK GLASS AND HARDWARE.** The prep work is the same for both windows and doors. Protect the surrounding area with disposable drop cloths. Clean the glass, then mask the glass perimeter and any nearby hardware with painter's tape. High-quality tapes may seem expensive, but they are less likely to leave a sticky residue.

2 **SCRAPE LOOSE PAINT.** Using a paint scraper or a painter's tool, scrape any loose paint. Sand out any scratches that don't reach the underlying surface.

3 **FILL DEEP SCRATCHES.** Two-part auto-body filler is great for repairing dog scratches and other deep imperfections. Apply it with a putty knife.

The weatherstripping on modern doors is generally easy to remove for painting. The vinyl-covered foam, sometimes identified as "Q-Lon" after one brand, is removed by starting at one end and gently pulling it out of the kerf that holds it. Removing the strip eliminates a lot of tedious masking. I replace it when the door is fully dry—24 hours for latex and about four days for oil It easily pushes back into the slot it came out of.

I recommend leaving hardware in place. Disassembly and keeping track of the many small parts is an unnecessary and sometimes expensive hassle. Asking a client to forgo doorknobs and locks for two or three days is an even bigger problem.

4 **SAND REPAIRS. Once it's dry (in about 15 minutes), sand the filler with 180-grit paper. Repairing significant damage may take more than one application.**

Choosing Paint

My favorite paint for interior work is Sherwin-Williams® ProClassic®. I like both latex- and oil-based versions. Most clients choose satin or semigloss, which are easy to keep clean but don't produce an overly shiny finish.

For new exterior work, I prefer slow-dry oil primers because they penetrate and stick well and they prevent brown stains caused by wood tannins. Slow-dry primers must dry for four days or more before a topcoat is applied. Otherwise, the evaporating solvents in the primer can cause blistering and poor adhesion of the topcoat.

For a topcoat on both new and old work, I use acrylic latex paint, such as Sherwin-Williams Duration® or Sherwin-Williams Emerald™. Acrylic latex paints have greater elasticity and are more vapor permeable than oil paints, which makes them better at dealing with seasonal moisture and wood movement.

The Right Equipment

For exterior painting on doors and windows, I like an angled-sash brush. For painting the interior of doors and windows, I like an "all-paints" nylon-bristle brush. Indoors,

Painting doors: start outside

1 **SPOT-PRIME AS NEEDED. Once any damage is repaired, lightly sand the rest of the door surface with 180-grit (exterior) or 220-grit (interior) paper. Cover repairs with stain-blocking oil-based primer. (Painting an entry door requires leaving it open for several hours. You'll need to manage small children and pets accordingly.) If the sun is directly on the door, open it fully so that it's shaded by the home's interior. Keeping the door cool prevents lap marks and deep brush marks.**

2 **REMOVE WEATHERSTRIPPING. Most exterior doors have kerf-in weatherstripping that's removed by gently pulling on it. Removing it eliminates a lot of tedious masking.**

STRAIN YOUR PAINT

  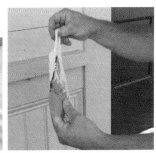

Old paint should be strained before use. Squeezing the paint through the strainer with a gloved hand saves time. Afterward, pull the glove off inside out to prevent a mess.

3 **APPLY THE FIRST COAT.** Starting at the top of the door, paint all of the rails and muntins, and then paint the stiles one at a time.

4 **APPLY THE SECOND COAT.** The second coat is applied in the same order as the first. For the second pass, though, remove the masking tape so that the paint laps onto the glass by about 1/16 in.

5 **CLEAN UP AS YOU GO.** Wipe off excess paint and drips right away. Remove masking materials when the paint is dry to the touch. Reinstall weatherstripping when the paint is fully dry (one day for latex; four days for oil).

where brushes don't get baked by the sun, I prefer nylon bristles because they shed less than other bristle types.

When I'm painting large areas such as stiles, rails, and panels, I dip one-third of the bristle length into the paint and then slap both sides of the brush on the inside of the paint pot. For smaller, more precise locations such as muntin bars, I dip the brush, slap the sides of the pot, and scrape both sides of the brush along the rim. This removes excess paint from the sides of the brush, helping to prevent drips at corners.

The Right Order

It's best to work from the inside out to prevent messing up work you've already completed. When painting the interior side of double-hung windows, I start with the upper sash; when working on the exterior side, I start with the lower sash. On doors, I start with the muntin bars and panels. Rails come next, and then the stiles. The edge of the door with hinges gets painted the exterior color. The latch edge is painted to match the door's interior side.

Philip Hansell (www.hansellpaint.com) is a professional painter in Durham, N.C.

Finish inside

1 **WORK FROM THE TOP DOWN.** After an initial sanding with 220-grit paper and a wipe-down with a tack cloth, paint the top rail and any muntin bars. Because this door was painted previously and was free of damage, priming was unnecessary. New doors and repaired areas should be primed before painting, however. (The panes of glass are completely taped over. I would not do this ordinarily, but the photographer was unable to get good pictures with the western sun streaming through the glass.)

2 **PANELS FIRST, STILES LAST.** Paint stiles one at a time. Brush away any drips where panels meet stiles and rails as soon as possible. Look for and correct drips near locks and hardware.

3 **SAND, TACK, AND RECOAT.** Sand the door with 320-grit paper, and wipe the surface clean with a tack cloth. Turn the cloth often to pick up the maximum amount of dust. Apply the second coat in the same order as the first. The inside of the door isn't exposed to weather, so you can leave the tape on the glass for both coats.

1 **LOWER THE UPPER SASH.** To paint a double-hung window correctly, you must be able to operate both sashes. You often can free a stuck sash by cutting the paint seal between it and the frame with a utility knife and then gently prying on the sash with a painter's tool or a small pry bar. Begin by painting the muntin bars on the top sash, then lower the sash to coat the bottom rail and the lowest part of the stiles.

2 **RAISE THE UPPER SASH.** Raise the upper sash and lower the bottom sash to expose the stiles and the top rail of the upper sash. Leave the sash partly open to paint the top rail.

3 **FINISH THE UPPER SASH.** Paint the top rail and then the stiles. A final pass with a dry (undipped) brush yields straight and uniform brush marks. Push up the painted sash with a painter's tool.

4 **PAINT THE BOTTOM SASH.** Working from the top down, paint the lower sash. Once you're done, brush out any drips where vertical and horizontal parts meet.

5 **PAINT THE TRIM.** Start with the head casing, and then paint the sides. Finish by coating the stool and the apron. As you finish each part, make a final pass with a dry brush.

10 Tips to Paint an Exterior Like a Pro

BY PHILIP HANSELL As a professional painter with nearly 20 years of experience, I've developed a thriving business. Getting there hasn't been easy, though, and I've made my share of mistakes. However, I've used these mistakes to improve my technique and to seek out high-quality, problem-solving products that I now rely on for almost every job. Here, I'll share some of my favorite products and some tips for getting the best possible exterior paint job.

The 2,200-sq.-ft. house featured here was in rough shape when we started, and it demonstrated that it's best not to neglect exterior painting for too long. Regular maintenance could have prevented much of the prep work and saved thousands of dollars when it came time to repaint. Because of the home's condition, we had between four and eight painters on the job for nearly two months, which pushed the clients' bill to more than $30,000. The price included removing the existing vinyl shutters; pressure-washing the entire house; scraping, priming, and painting all the trim and overhangs; stripping much of the siding down to bare wood; and painting the porches, siding, and window sashes. Finally, we painted and hung new, historically accurate wooden shutters.

In April 2008, the EPA released new rules for painting and remodeling houses that have lead-based paint. If you're a contractor and you're caught ignoring the EPA's RRP (renovation, repair, and painting) rule, you're risking your livelihood. One Connecticut-based company was fined more than $30,000 for violations. Homeowners doing their own work are exempt, but that doesn't mean they should disregard the requirements. If you're a homeowner planning to repaint your own house, I suggest reading up or taking a class on handling lead-based paint.

TIP 1

Scrape and sand before washing

When there is a lot of scraping and sanding to do, as there was on the house featured here, we like to do it before the house is washed. Many painters make the mistake of washing first and then doing a lot of heavy sanding afterward. The dust left behind makes it hard for the paint to bond. After the scraping and sanding are done and the house has been washed, check all scraped areas to make sure the washing didn't loosen any more paint.

TIP 2

Stick to low pressure when washing

We add about a tablespoon of dish soap to our mix of trisodium phosphate (TSP) and bleach. Dish soap creates suds that help the solution to cling to the siding and trim instead of running off the house. Then we rinse the house with a pressure washer on a low setting. Never use high pressure, which can force water into the wood and damage siding and windows.

SCRAPE FIRST. Saving the washing until after scraping and sanding will remove dust that could prevent the paint from bonding well.

TIP 3

Cover plants, cars, and exterior light fixtures

We use lightweight canvas drop cloths to cover plants. They don't break branches, and they let the plants breathe. Plastic covers can heat up like a greenhouse and kill plants. We cover lights, windows, and doors with ClingCover™ plastic. Unlike with traditional poly sheeting, tape sticks well to the slightly textured surface. This material comes in 9-ft. by 400-ft. rolls. Automobile covers are one of those touches that show our clients we do quality work and care about their possessions.

TIP 4

Consider special primers instead of whole-house paint removal

If we are working on a house that has old oil-based paint that is peeling and cracking badly and complete removal is not an option, we like to use XIM Peel Bond™ primer. It's a high-build, clear acrylic primer that can be applied up to 30 mils thick. It's great at leveling cracked surfaces, and it costs two-thirds less than stripping down to bare wood. We used this product on the porch ceilings and on the second story of the house shown here as a way to make the project more affordable. We stripped the lower part of the house down to bare wood so that it would have a flawless finish at eye level.

COVER IT UP. Taking the time to mask and protect the surrounding area (including any cars nearby) is a sure sign of a professional paint job.

TAKE LEAD SERIOUSLY. Professionals must follow the EPA's RRP rule for dealing with lead-based paint. Although homeowners are legally exempt, they should still take the necessary precautions.

TIP 5

The right tool makes all the difference

With the EPA's RRP rule for dealing with lead-based paint in effect, we had to rethink how to prepare surfaces that test positive for lead. When we were introduced to a sander/vacuum combo by a local cabinet builder, I was really impressed, but I was hesitant to buy one because of the price. The vac's EPA-approved HEPA filter captures 99.97% of particles down to 0.3 microns. We love that these vacuums protect our employees from lead exposure and reduce our cleanup time. In fact, we like them so much that we plan to buy six more this year.

SOMETIMES YOU HAVE TO START FROM SCRATCH

On old houses, paint can be in such rough shape that complete removal is the only way to go. We like a stripping product called Peel Away®, which has the consistency of joint compound (**1**). We apply it with a mud knife in a ¼-in.- to ⅝-in.-thick coat (**2**), then cover it with the waxy paper included with the product (**3**). We leave it covered for 12 to 72 hours, checking it about three times a day until we see that it has worked its way through all the layers of paint. After scraping off the softened paint onto 6-mil plastic with a putty or taping knife (**4**), we apply with pump sprayers the neutralizer that comes with the product (**5**). We work it in with stiff nylon brushes, let the wood dry for a couple of days, then neutralize and scrub again. The final step is a scrub and rinse with clear water. After the wood is dry, we check the pH with a test strip. If the pH is too high, we go through the neutralization process again. Once neutralization is complete, it's important to check the wood's moisture content before priming. Anything below 15% is acceptable. Peel Away is labor intensive, but when done correctly, it gives great results. On this house, we used it on the siding up to the bottom of the second-story windows.

Pick the right primer

With so many primers out there, it's easy to get confused about which one to use. We almost always use a slow-drying oil-based primer for exterior wood, such as Sherwin-Williams' Exterior Oil-Based Wood Primer. Because it dries slowly, it has time to penetrate the wood and provides the best base for all types of paint. Many people think that if they are going to use latex paint, then they must use latex primer, which is incorrect. As long as the primer has time to dry, it's perfectly fine to top-coat with latex paint. For fiberglass and PVC trim that needs to be painted, we've had good success with Sherwin-Williams' Adhesion Primer. One often-overlooked step is to wipe these materials with denatured alcohol to remove any manufacturing oils before priming. When priming new wood, watch out for mill glaze. I've heard carpenters and painters say they don't believe in mill glaze, but if the wood appears shiny or especially smooth or if it's been in the sun for a few weeks, sand it lightly before priming.

DO THE PREP WORK. Before priming, any loose glazing putty and peeling paint must be removed, and the new glazing must be allowed to dry.

TIP 7

Allow extra time for painting windows

When painting old windows, it's best to remove loose glazing putty and peeling paint and then reglaze where needed. It's OK to leave portions of old glazing putty if they're well adhered. Once the glazing putty is dry (we like to wait two to three weeks), we mask the perimeter of the window with 1½-in.-wide blue tape, which protects the glass from scratches and speeds up priming and painting. After masking, we sand all the wood and old glazing, then wash the window with a solution of TSP, bleach, and detergent. We let it sit for 10 to 15 minutes, then rinse the window with clear water. After the window is dry, we prime the sash and glazing putty with a slow-drying oil-based primer. Once the primer is dry, we sand the wood lightly, caulk where needed, and apply the first coat of paint. Then we pull off the tape and clean the glass with spray-on glass cleaner and paper towels. For the final coat, we lap the paint ¹⁄₁₆ in. onto the glass. This prevents water from getting behind the glazing putty, which is what causes the putty to fail. Before the paint dries, we open and close the window a few times to prevent it from becoming sealed shut with paint.

SASHES MUST LOOK GOOD INSIDE AND OUT. The last step in painting windows is to scrape excess paint from the glass and to give it a thorough cleaning. If the window sticks because of the recent paint job, the sides of the frame are given a coat of paste wax.

WINDOWS GET EXTRA ATTENTION. With the glazing putty replaced and the window scraped and primed, the author's crew fills screw holes left by the old shutters with auto-body filler. The patches are then sanded with 150-grit paper and primed.

PAINT IN THE RIGHT ORDER

Sometimes it's hard to know where to start on an exterior paint job. Below are outlines that show how we paint homes in good condition and homes that have been neglected.

HOME WITH MINOR PEELING

1. Remove the shutters and screens.
2. Wash the exterior, shutters, and screens.
3. Scrape all loose paint and glazing putty.
4. Replace any rotten wood.
5. Sand all scraped areas.
6. Spot-prime all bare wood.
7. Apply caulk and glazing putty where needed.
8. Brush all overhangs and high trim.
9. Paint all siding.
10. Paint the windows, doors, and trim.
11. Paint the porch floors.
12. Hang the shutters and screens.

HOME WITH MAJOR PEELING

1. Remove the shutters and screens.
2. Scrape all loose paint and glazing putty.
3. Sand where needed.
4. Wash the exterior, shutters, and screens.
5. Check the scraped areas, and sand where needed.
6. Replace any rotten wood.
7. Prime all wood.
8. Apply caulk and glazing putty where needed.
9. Paint all shutters.
10. Brush all overhangs and high trim.
11. Paint all siding.
12. Paint the windows, doors, and trim.
13. Paint the porch floors.
14. Hang the shutters and screens.

TIP 8

Wrap up painting by early afternoon in the fall and spring

Surfactant leaching is something that most people haven't heard about but have probably seen. It occurs when ingredients in the paint leach to the surface as a result of moisture. It's common in the fall and spring with their warm days and cool nights. At night, condensation forms on the paint film, then the water breaks down the water-soluble components in the paint and brings them to the surface. When the water evaporates, it leaves behind a waxy-looking area that usually wears off on its own, but it's hard to convince a customer of this. To prevent surfactant leaching, we stop painting around 1 p.m. in the spring and fall. We do surface prep in the early morning, paint from late morning to shortly after lunch, and then resume prep work until the end of the day. This process takes longer, but it avoids problems.

DIY ONE SIDE AT A TIME

If you are a homeowner trying to tackle a large exterior paint job yourself, my first advice is to set plenty of short-term goals. If you set out to paint the exterior of your house without a plan, you're going to run out of steam or end up hating painting. I recommend working on one side of the house at a time, preferably starting on the least visible elevation. This will give you time to develop your technique and to perfect your painting skills. If you're like me, there are probably a few projects around the house that you haven't finished, so you don't want to add exterior painting to the list.

With such a long-term project, you're likely to get rained out on occasion. I suggest keeping some work in reserve, such as prepping and painting shutters and sashes, that you can do in the garage or basement on rainy days. Make sure to protect yourself and your family from lead paint by avoiding any dry-sanding or scraping and by keeping a neat work area free of paint chips.

If you are going to try Peel Away, do a test spot first because sometimes it works in hours and sometimes it takes days. Don't apply more than you can remove in one day. Letting the wood sit bare for a couple of months isn't a problem unless you live in an area with a lot of rainfall. If the wood is going to be bare for weeks or months, tack up some 6-mil plastic to protect it. When we need to protect bare siding from rain, we wrap the plastic around a 2x4 and screw it to the house. We keep the plastic rolled up as much as possible so that the wood under it can dry, and we let it down only when there is a good chance of rain.

HOW TO TACKLE A DIY WHOLE-HOUSE PAINT JOB

1. Remove all shutters and storm windows or screens.
2. Remove all loose window glazing.
3. Glaze the windows where needed.
4. Scrape and sand the overhangs.
5. Wash and prime the overhangs.
6. Scrape and sand the siding.
7. Wash and prime the siding.
8. Scrape and sand the windows, doors, and trim.
9. Wash and prime the windows, doors, and trim.
10. Scrape and sand the shutters.
11. Wash the shutters.
12. Prime and paint the shutters.
13. Caulk.
14. Paint the overhangs.
15. Paint the siding.
16. Paint the windows, doors, and trim.
17. Clean the windows.
18. Hang the storm windows or screens.
19. Hang the shutters.

There's a quick fix for sticky doors and windows

Have you ever tried to open a cabinet door that feels like it is glued shut? This condition is known as blocking, and it is common on places where cured latex paint tries to stick to itself, such as on wood windows, painted doors without weatherstripping, and garage doors. Most exterior paints are not resistant to blocking, so we apply a thin coat of clear Briwax® to window sashes, garage-door panels, and places where doors meet door stops.

TIP 10

Don't forget home maintenance

Most people think that if they clean their gutters twice a year, they've maintained their home. We recommend that our customers hire us to wash their homes every other year and to have us check the caulking and touch up the paint where needed. We have customers who have 11-year-old paint jobs that look nearly new. The cost for this service is usually under $1,000 and can add years to a paint job. I've seen something simple like cracked caulking between trim and a windowsill ruin many window frames. These costly repairs could have been avoided with a $10 tube of caulk and a few minutes of work.

Philip Hansell (www.hansellpaint.com) is a professional painter in Durham, N.C.

KEEP IT UP. Caulking and touch-up paint can maintain a paint job for years, while neglect can lead to a costly redo much sooner.

INTERIOR SOLUTIONS

Cutting a Laminate Countertop for a Sink

BY ANDY ENGEL ▓ When you're building or remodeling a kitchen, you can save time and money by using a ready-made laminate countertop. These tops, which generally have an integral backsplash and wraparound front edge, are durable and easy to find at home centers and lumberyards. Even if you have a laminate top custom-fabricated or you make it yourself, you can still use the sink-cutting methods described here.

Many sinks come with a layout template that makes marking the cut easy; you just trace the template with a pencil and cut out the hole with a jigsaw. If you don't have a template, trace around the sink rim with a pencil, and then adjust the line inward to get the proper fit. On dark tops like this one, I make the layout marks on light-colored masking tape so they're easier to see.

I cut most of the opening with a jigsaw equipped with a laminate-cutting blade. These blades cut on the downstroke to prevent chipping. If the countertop has an integral backsplash, there's usually not enough room for a jigsaw when making the rear cut (adjacent to the backsplash). I make this cut with an oscillating multitool.

After making the rear cut, I attach a cleat to the cutout with a single screw. The cleat supports the cutout in place to prevent the countertop from breaking as the cut is finished. I use one screw so I can rotate the cleat out of the blade's path while cutting.

To make less mess, you might be tempted to cut the top outdoors or in your shop and then move the prepared top to the sink base. I generally don't do this because with a large hole in the center, it's very easy to break the countertop while moving it.

Andy Engel is a senior *Fine Homebuilding* editor.

1 **CENTER THE SINK.** Use a combination square lined up between the cabinet doors to establish the side-to-side location of the sink. Make sure the front cut won't hit the cabinet rail below.

2 **TRACE THE LINE.** Trace the template or the sink rim as the starting point for layout lines. A layer of tape helps you see the pencil lines.

3 **MOVE THE LINE INWARD.** Without a template, the layout line must be moved inward so it will be covered by the sink rim. The margins vary by sink, but the minimum is about ¼ in. Make a mark at both ends of all four sides.

4 **CONNECT THE DOTS.** Use a straightedge to connect the marks that correspond with the actual cutline. Connect the corners at an angle for an easier cut and better sink support.

5 **DOUBLE-CHECK THE LAYOUT.** Confirm that the cuts will be covered fully by the sink rim, then cross out the original lines to prevent cutting on the wrong line.

CONTINUED ON PAGE 42 ▶

CONTINUED FROM PAGE 41

6 **DRILL THE CORNERS.** Drill the insides of every corner with a ³⁄₈-in. spade bit. Make sure the holes are fully within the lines that mark the actual sink cutout.

7 **CUT THE BACK.** Because of the backsplash, there's generally not enough room to cut the back side with a jigsaw. Instead, use a fine-tooth blade in an oscillating multitool.

8 **ATTACH A CLEAT.** To prevent the top from breaking as you finish the cut, secure a cleat to the top. A single screw in the center allows you to rotate the cleat out of the way while cutting.

9 **FINISH UP WITH A JIGSAW.** Use a jigsaw with a reverse-cutting blade to finish the sink cutout. Maintain downward pressure to keep the saw from bouncing as it cuts.

10 **TEST THE FIT.** After checking that the sink fits inside the cutout, clean all dust from the countertop, run a bead of silicone sealant around the rim, and install the clips that secure the sink.

MAKE THE CUT

To prevent damaging the laminate countertop, use a reverse-cutting jigsaw blade. These blades have teeth that cut on the downstroke instead of the upstroke. Go slowly, and apply steady downward pressure so that the saw doesn't bounce while cutting.

There's often not enough room to fit a jigsaw between the back of the sink and the backsplash. In these instances, use a fine-tooth blade in an oscillating multitool (photo left). Make the cut in several passes so you don't overheat the blade, which slows cutting and dulls the teeth.

Coping Moldings

BY TOM O'BRIEN When two pieces of trim meet at an inside corner, you could miter the joint, but most professional carpenters prefer to cope. An airtight coped joint is easier to produce: It doesn't require the perfectly square corner that a mitered joint needs. A coped joint is also less likely to open up after a few seasons of expansion and contraction.

Although you need a miter saw for coping, the only specialty tools you need are a coping saw and an assortment of blades. A 15-tooth coping-saw blade is the best all-around performer, especially for simple chair rails and baseboards. But you'll want 18 teeth (or more) to negotiate the intricate cuts that crown molding requires.

When installing a new blade, make sure the teeth face forward (the same as a standard handsaw) and tighten the blade securely.

Tom O'Brien is a carpenter in New Milford, Conn., and a former *Fine Homebuilding* editor.

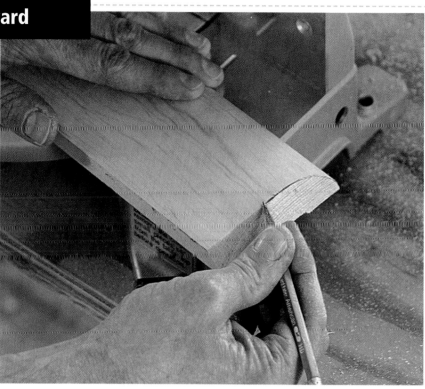

1 **MITER CUT DETERMINES THE PROFILE.** Although you can trace the profile from one piece of trim to the other, a 45° inside miter cut achieves the same purpose. An efficient carpenter chops all the profiles for a particular room at the same time, then cuts each piece of trim to length later.

2 **USE A PENCIL TO HIGHLIGHT THE CUTLINE.** To make the profile of the molding more apparent, draw the flat edge of a pencil lead across the inside edge of the miter cut.

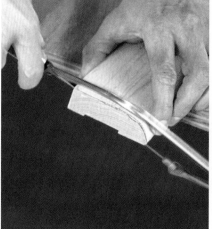

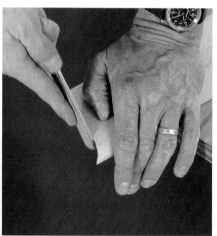

3 **ANGLE THE CUT INWARD.** Start the cut with a few gentle pull strokes until the coping saw finds its groove, then switch to long push strokes.

4 **ANGLE THE BLADE INTO THE WORK** so that the face of the cut becomes slightly proud of the back side. This slight angle is called a back bevel, or back cut.

5 **THE BACK BEVEL ALLOWS MINOR ADJUSTMENTS** to be accomplished using a few passes with a wood rasp rather than a belt sander.

TURN YOUR JIGSAW INTO A SUPERCHARGED COPING SAW

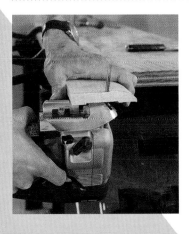

If you measure your trim in miles rather than feet, you might want to invest in the Collins Coping Foot (www.collinstool.com). The coping foot is simply a curved baseplate that substitutes for the standard, flat base found on a typical jigsaw. The manufacturer offers a coping foot to fit all commercially available jigsaws. Most install with the turn of a screw, though some saws require a shim to position the baseplate correctly.

With the coping foot in place, the saw is operated upside down, which takes a little practice but allows you to see the cutline perfectly. The curved base makes it easy to back-bevel a baseboard, but it was designed for quickly negotiating the intricate twists and turns that crown molding requires. Instructions for coping crown using a simple jig are included with the tool.

Crown takes patience and a steady hand

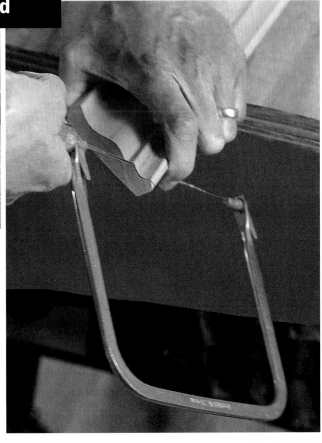

1 PLACE THE CROWN MOLDING UPSIDE DOWN in the miter saw and at an angle between the fence and base. Then make a 45° cut to reveal the profile for the cope.

2 CROWN NEEDS A STEEP BACK BEVEL. Because it's installed on an angle, unlike baseboard, crown molding must be coped with a significant back bevel, or the two faces won't meet.

CONTINUED ON PAGE 46 ▶

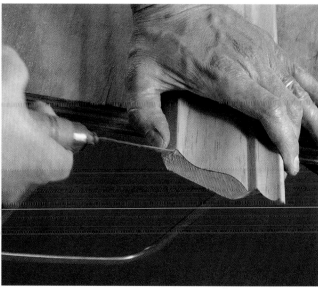

3 **IT'S NOT EASY TO TURN CORNERS** when sawing at such a steep angle, so the best strategy is to cut as far as you can from one end, back the blade out, and sneak up on the cut from another direction.

4 **WORK INWARD FROM BOTH EDGES** to ensure that the last saw stroke separates the meaty center of the molding rather than the fragile outer edge.

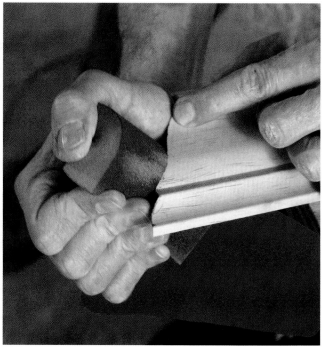

5 **CLOSE WON'T DO.** If the cope doesn't fit perfectly, a pencil serves to mark the high spots, which are removed easily with a rasp or some sandpaper.

6 **FINE-TUNE THE CURVES.** A medium-grit sanding sponge is particularly effective for shaping curved sections.

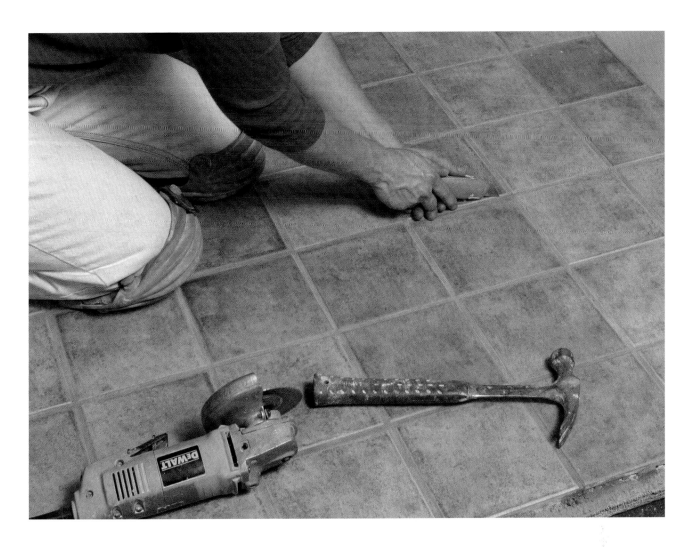

Replacing a Broken Tile

BY JANE AEON ▨ It was bound to happen. The new floors have been finished for less than a week, and someone already has dropped a hammer on the kitchen's tile floor. Unless the tile guy is still on the job, you're either going to wait a long time or fix it yourself.

Luckily, it's a fairly easy fix, as long as you use the right technique. Although you can use a hammer and an old chisel to break out the damaged tile, this technique can be risky. Within grout joints tighter than 3/16 in., hammer blows can chip or crack adjacent tiles. Hammering also can pulverize the substrate beneath the damaged tile.

Occasionally, I use a hole saw to cut out the center portion of a cracked tile. This technique is good for removing soft-bodied tile. It's usually a slow process, but I'm left with a hole in the tile that makes it easy to pry with the tip of a chisel or a screwdriver.

My preferred technique, however, is to use an angle grinder outfitted with a 4-in. diamond blade and a shop vacuum. This technique is good for thick, soft-bodied tiles such as saltillo, but it works on others as well. The tile must be larger than 4 in., or there won't be room for a 4-in. grinder blade.

Basically, the trick is first to isolate the tile from neighboring tiles by removing the surrounding grout line, then carefully break the tile into pieces and remove it. Using a grinder can be messy unless you keep a vacuum nozzle trained on the dust stream. I mask off any surrounding cabinet faces or furniture and also protect neighboring tiles with sheet metal or plywood in case I overcut. I mask off myself as well, donning safety glasses, a dust mask, and hearing protection.

I start by making diagonal cuts, then make separate cuts that run parallel to the edges. The parallel cuts along the tile edges make it possible to position a chisel from the edge of a tile facing in so that the neighboring tile is not damaged. This technique is good for removing tiles with tight joints, like marble. A cordless 3⅜-in. saw with a slightly smaller diamond blade comes in handy; I also use a rotary tool fitted with a small diamond-point bit in the corners where the grinder can't reach.

Once the tile is removed, I scrape out any remaining thinset and vacuum the substrate. With fresh thinset and a new tile, the job is finished, except for the grouting work.

Jane Aeon is a former tile contractor in Berkeley, Calif.

1 **ISOLATE THE VICTIM.** To keep the neighboring tiles intact, the first step is to score the grout lines with a utility knife. A few light passes do the trick.

2 **PROTECTION IS PREVENTION.** Before cutting, it's a good idea to mask off any nearby cabinets or furniture with plastic and tape. On the floor, angle brackets taped to the surrounding tiles protect them from inadvertent slips of the grinder's blade.

3 **DIAGONAL CUTS OPEN UP THE TILE.** With both hands firmly holding the grinder, the author carefully plunges the blade into the tile's center and cuts diagonally, then along the tile's sides. A helper holds the vacuum hose to catch the dusty exhaust.

4 **A JUNKY TOOL STILL HAS ITS USES.** Using a hammer and an old chisel or putty knife, the author works from the outside toward the tile's center, carefully prying out the pieces.

6 **BACK TO SQUARE ONE, AGAIN.** After making sure the replacement tile fits, the author mixes a small batch of thinset, trowels it into the space (left), and sets the tile. After the thinset dries, the tile can be grouted.

5 **MAKE A CLEAR SPACE.** After the tile is removed, all old thinset and grout are scraped from the substrate, which then is vacuumed clean.

Perfecting the Tiled Tub Surround

BY TOM MEEHAN ■ Over my 35 years of installing tile, I've done well over a thousand tub surrounds. Take it from me: Tiling a tub surround might seem like the kind of remodeling project you can jump right into, but it's not.

It takes quite a bit of planning and proper follow-through to get quality results. To this day, I still treat each new installation the same as the first. The key lies in knowing how the last tile will fit before the first tile touches the wall. This means knowing how well the tub was installed, where each course of tile will land, and how the cut tiles will lay out.

For this job, the customer asked for classic 3x5 white subway tile, which has never gone out of style in all the years I've been on the job. To give the tub surround a bit of a kick, I incorporated a band of mosaic tile into the layout and installed a marble corner shelf for shampoo bottles and a bar of soap. Neither of these little changes added much cost for materials or much time to the installation, but both help this space to stand apart from a typical tiled tub surround.

As is the case in any wet area, the tile substrate should be cement backerboard or another approved backer that will not deteriorate or harbor mold. In this case, because the tub surround met wall paneling on one side, I used standard ½-in.-thick Durock® cementboard for most of the job, but installed ¼-in.-thick HardieBacker® board, a fiber-cement product, on the wall that needed to be flush to the paneling.

Strategies for Success

I start all of my installations by making a story pole to help me in planning the horizontal and vertical layout. On the back wall of the tub, which is seen first and most frequently, I want the tiles laid out so that any necessary cuts land in the two corners and are of equal size. On the sidewalls, where symmetry is not as important, cuts can be hidden in the back corners.

If the tile will stop short of the ceiling, then you won't need to cut the top row. I usually run my tub surrounds right to the ceiling. I'd rather not end up with a small piece at the top, but I also want a full tile at the tub. Determining the size of each course can require a little compromise. If it looks as though the course of tile at the ceiling will be too narrow, I try reducing the size of the pieces on top of the tub. Also, if the tub is significantly out of level, a line of cut tile at the tub will make the problem less obvious. On the job shown here, the tub was out of level by about ¼ in. from end to end, which is a very common situation. I accounted for this by planning the bottom row so that full-height tile starts at the lowest point and is gradually adjusted and cut as needed to absorb the high spots.

1 **A STORY POLE ELIMINATES SURPRISES. Unless you're really lucky, you'll have to cut some tiles to make the layout work. The key is planning where those cuts should land so that they are less noticeable. Cut tiles should be no less than half the size of a full tile. Sometimes small pieces are unavoidable, but the problem can be minimized with a little effort and imagination. To start, cut a piece of wood for the vertical layout and another for the horizontal layout, each a bit shorter than the distance between tub and ceiling or wall and wall. Place the tiles one at a time, including a space for grout between each if the tile isn't self-spacing, and mark the layout on the stick.** CONTINUED ON PAGE 52

CONTINUED FROM PAGE 51

2 **KNOW YOUR TUB INSTALLATION.** It would be nice if every tub installation were dead level, but that's rarely the case. Before you can begin the tile layout, lay a level across the top of each side of the tub. The bottom row of tiles can be cut to follow the contour of the tub or to account for high spots, so the goal here is to find the low point, which becomes the starting point for the rest of the layout.

3 **UP FROM THE BOTTOM.** Set the end of the story pole on the tub's lowest spot, then draw a mark at least halfway up the wall that corresponds to the joints of your story-pole layout.

Gap shows how much will need to be cut from the top row of tile.

4 **ESTABLISH A BENCHMARK.** Transfer the halfway mark across all three walls of the tub surround, making sure it's level. This is your benchmark line.

5 **PLAN FOR THE BAND.** It's also a good idea to use the story pole to determine the position of the accent band and the way it will relate to the shower hardware, as well as the position of niches or shelves in the tub surround.

6 **FLIP IT FOR THE CEILING.** Turned end for end and placed against the ceiling, the story pole indicates the amount that needs to be cut from the top row. Here, the cut will leave almost an entire tile, which is perfect.

Installing Tile Is the Fun Part

Once the layout has been determined, the hard part of the job is just about done. There will still be some tiles that need to be cut and some holes to be made for plumbing, but as long as you follow the plan and keep the tiles level, the next step will be the fast and gratifying part of the installation.

I always spread an ample amount of cement to get a full bond rather than skimping and leaving a few voids on the wall. When there's a good coating of thinset on the wall, I comb it with the teeth of the trowel in one direction. This makes a big difference in achieving a complete bond. Making sure that trowel lines all go in one direction reduces the possibility of voids in the thinset behind the tile. I also make sure to push each tile into the cement and give it a ¼-in. slide to achieve a good bond. Subway tiles often have self-spacing nibs to keep grout joints consistent.

Regardless of the tile, though, you should always check with a level to ensure that the tiles are running at the same height and that joints are lining up at the corners.

I usually tile the lower half of all three walls of a tub surround before moving any higher. A pro can install about 25 sq. ft. of tile in 20 to 30 minutes. If you're a DIYer, plan on no more than half that square footage.

Cutting the tiles is the hard part of the job. The cut pieces have to fit properly and the grout joints should be spaced evenly so that everything blends together smoothly. Most ceramic, porcelain, and even some glass tiles can be cut with a snap cutter, which is a fast, portable, and nearly silent tool. Notches, curves, and other fairly simple nonlinear cuts can be handled with a pair of nippers. Almost all stone tiles, and even some handmade tiles, have to be cut with a wet saw, which is also indispensable for more complicated cuts or when working with fragile tiles.

1 **INSTALLATION STARTS WITH THE BOTTOM HALF.** With the layout established, the tiles go up quickly. Work the bottom half of the installation first, starting with the back wall and then tiling each of the sidewalls. Working from the benchmark line down, spread the thinset cement with a ¼-in. square-notched trowel. Use a sag-resistant latex-modified thinset such as Laticrete® 255 for tub surrounds because it reduces the chance that tiles will slide out of position before the cement sets up. Simple straight cuts can be made as you go, but tile as much as possible before slowing down to make the more complicated cuts, like those around plumbing fixtures.

2 **THE FIRST TILE ESTABLISHES THE PATTERN.** On this job, the story pole confirmed that a full row of uncut tiles could fit along the back wall, so the first row begins with a full tile, followed by a half-tile below it to establish the running bond pattern. If a full row of uncut tile won't fit, it's better to start in the center of the wall and have the same cut on each end.

CONTINUED ON PAGE 54 ▶

CONTINUED FROM PAGE 53

3 **SCORE AND SNAP.** For all straight cuts, a basic snap cutter works quickly and makes a clean cut. Score across the top of the tile, then give the handle a quick bump with the palm of your hand to break the tile at the score line. If the cuts are difficult, small, or notched, a tile saw is a better choice.

4 **CURVES REQUIRE NIPPERS.** After installing as many full tiles as possible around the showerhead and mixing valve, you can use a pair of nippers to fit in the remaining tiles. Holding the tile in place, use a permanent marker to outline the area that needs to be cut. Carefully nibble up to the marked line with a set of tile nippers. The cuts don't have to be pretty; just get close enough so that the tile easily fits the open spot in the layout. The gap will be covered by the fixture's trim plate.

5 **KEEPING CUTS TO THE BOTTOM.** Compensate for an out-of-level tub at the bottom row of tile. After using a straightedge to ensure that the highest completed row is straight, fill in the tiles at the tub. These cuts, which are often tapered and can vary from tile to tile, can be done on a snap cutter, but a wet saw is more accurate.

2 **SPREAD AND SCRAPE.**
Use a margin trowel
to load grout onto a rubber
float, and then use the float
to apply it to the wall. Spread
the grout in broad, arcing
strokes. Start with your arm
extended, and pull the float
toward your body. The first
pass packs grout into the
joints; the second pass scrapes
away most of the excess.

3 **PACK AND TOOL THE JOINTS.** Once the grout has
firmed up but before you wash down the tile,
use the butt end of a Sharpie® permanent marker as a
grout stick to strike the grout joints. This packs in the
grout tightly and makes the joint consistent.

4 **WIPE AWAY THE HAZE.** Once the tile has been
washed down and all excess grout removed, let
everything dry for about 15 minutes, or until a light
haze develops on the surface of the tile. Then use a
clean cloth or quality paper towel to wipe the haze off
the surface of the tile, buffing it to a finished shine.

Fixing Wood-Floor Flaws

BY CHARLES PETERSON ■ I love the look and durability of wood floors, and it's not just because I've been installing them since 1978. I'm impressed by a surface that receives such a tremendous amount of abuse yet—if properly installed and cared for—can last as long as a house.

Still, wood floors are hardly indestructible: Every year, an estimated $1 billion worth of hardwood-floor damage occurs across the country.

As a consultant and author for the National Wood Flooring Association (www.woodfloors.org), I've made it my business to understand what causes all that damage, as well as how to fix it. Here are nine common floor flaws, why they occur, and what you can do.

Abnormal Gaps

Wood floors are prone to movement. Installed correctly, floorboards hold tight to one another during humid times of the year and might reveal gaps during drier times. Abnormal gaps are generally the result of flooring that's too wet when it is installed, but they also can be the consequence of installing flooring in areas of excessive dryness, such as directly over heating ducts or in areas that receive a lot of sunlight.

What to do

Gaps are an aesthetic issue and should be repaired when they disrupt the overall look of a floor, not when they measure a particular width. Repair them at the most humid time of year, when they are at their smallest. If you repair gaps when they are at their widest, you might not leave sufficient clearance between floorboards and create a floor that buckles when it expands.

To repair gaps, make a patch by gluing thin strips of wood to the edges of the floorboards. Be careful to apply glue to only one side of the strip so that you don't glue any boards together.

NOT ALL GAPS ARE BAD, BUT THESE ARE. The gaps pictured here are too big and irregular. They take away from the overall look of the floor, which should be relatively uniform across its surface.

Cupping

When the bottom of a board is wetter than the top, the edges cup. Wide-plank floors are more prone to cupping, but I've seen it happen to strip flooring as well. Most often, cupping happens when flooring is installed over a wet basement or crawlspace.

What to do

First, take whatever measures are necessary to eliminate the moisture problem. Some cupped floors lie flat once moisture issues are corrected. Other floors might be deformed permanently. A floor that doesn't lie flat needs to be sanded, but only when the moisture content of the top and bottom of the boards is within 1%. Drive a moisture meter through the subfloor to check the bottoms of the boards. If you sand the peaked edges of a cupped floor too soon, you could have crowned boards when they're fully dry.

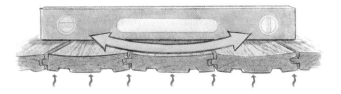

CUPPING. The edges of floor boards will curl up if the bottom of a board is wetter than the top.

BOARDS BUCKLE IF THEY CAN'T EXPAND. When floorboards aren't acclimated or are exposed to lots of moisture, they can crush together and lift off the subfloor.

Buckling

When wood flooring becomes too moist, it can expand to the point that it lifts off the subfloor, moves door frames, and pops trim from the wall. A floor can buckle because of a damp basement, because of a flood, or because the floor was installed when it was too dry. Improper fastening can aggravate the condition: Nails might be the wrong size or might be spaced too far apart. On glue-down installations, using the wrong size trowel can lead to a poor bond between the floorboards and the subfloor.

What to do

Some buckled floors can be refastened, while others have to be removed. Reuse floorboards when possible, but if the tongues and grooves are torn apart or if the boards are cracked, replace them. Don't repair buckled floors until the moisture problems in the house have been fixed.

Peeling Finish

Floor finishes peel because the floor was contaminated or improperly prepped when the finish was applied. Excessive sanding with high-grit paper can burnish wood and create a surface too smooth for the finish to adhere. Inadequate abrading or cleaning between finish coats, applying a topcoat over a floor that is not dry, or working with incompatible finishes all can cause peeling. However, the most common cause of peeling is stain residue that isn't cleaned from the floor prior to applying finish.

What to do

The best way to fix a peeling floor is to sand it down to bare wood and restart the finishing process. Simply abrading the floor and applying a new topcoat might not fix the problem. Without resanding, the waxes, oils, and furniture polishes used to clean wood floors seep into the pores of the finish and can prevent the new finish from bonding successfully.

A CONTAMINATED FLOOR WON'T HOLD FINISH. Dirt or chemicals on top of a floor or embedded in its finish can cause subsequent coats of finish to flake or peel off.

Excessive Wear

All wood floors eventually wear out, but when they're in rough shape after only a couple of years, it's likely that the floor wasn't sanded properly, the finish was poorly applied, or the floor wasn't maintained well. Even when sanded and finished properly, wood requires regular maintenance. Grit left on wood floors acts like sandpaper when walked on, and unclipped pet nails or unprotected furniture feet can scratch a finish considerably.

What to do

You might be able to recoat a slightly worn floor without sanding off all the old finish. But when a floor has lots of wear and deep scratches, it's best to sand down the floor to bare wood and refinish it.

DON'T ALWAYS BLAME THE DOG FOR FAST-WEARING FLOORS. A worn floor lacks sheen and evenness in color. Poor finishing techniques can be the cause as much as family pets and household abuse.

Debris in the Finish

Wet finish acts like a large piece of flypaper. Any dust or animal hair that finds its way into it will be magnified once the finish is dry.

What to do

The best way to keep debris from marring your floor's finish is to keep it from getting there in the first place. To prevent debris from ruining the finish, clean all the room's surfaces prior to finishing the floor. Wipe down the walls and light fixtures. Then vacuum the floor and go over it with a tack cloth. (Don't use tack cloths designed for use on cars; they can contain silicone, which will compromise the finish.) I recommend straining the finish and pouring it into an applicator tray lined with an inside-out garbage bag. Remove any loose fibers from the applicator by washing and vacuuming it thoroughly.

If debris does find its way into the finish, sand the floor as you would between coats of finish and apply a new topcoat.

Sanding Blemishes

Worn abrasive screens or sanding pads used to sand between coats of finish can create unsightly scratches in the floor. Subsequent coats of finish magnify these imperfections.

What to do

To remove the scratches, you'll have to sand the finish past the coat where the scratches were initially made. That's often difficult to pinpoint, so I tend to sand off all the finish and start again.

To prevent these scratches from recurring, use high-quality abrasive pads when sanding between each coat. They leave smaller, more plentiful but less noticeable scratches, and also create a scratch pattern that promotes a much better adhesion between coats of finish. I like to use 150-grit to 180-grit pads when sanding oil-based polyurethanes and 220 grit when sanding between coats of water-based finishes.

FINISHES ENHANCE THE BAD AS MUCH AS THE GOOD. Debris on the floor surface or in the finish, such as this hair, is magnified when the finish is dry.

SLOPPY SANDING SHOWS. Using a worn sanding screen to sand between coats can leave spiderweb-like defects in the finish.

REPLACING A DAMAGED FLOORBOARD

Measure the new board by lining it up with the damaged one, and mark it carefully with a knife blade (far right). Then remove the bottom of the groove from the new board on a tablesaw (near right). This allows the board to slip over the tongue of the adjacent floorboard.

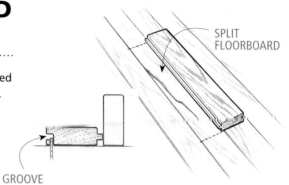

SPLIT FLOORBOARD

GROOVE

1 **BEVEL THE ENDS OF THE NEW BOARD.** This step provides for a snug fit with the adjacent floorboards.

2 **REMOVE THE DAMAGED BOARD.** Drill holes near the edge of the damaged board, and use a jigsaw to crosscut it. With a circular saw, make two cuts down the length of the board.

3 **USE A CHISEL.** Remove the pieces, working away from the undamaged floorboards.

4 **INSTALL THE NEW BOARD.** First, drive the old nails into the subfloor, and then make sure the subfloor is absolutely clean with no high spots. Glue in the new board using construction adhesive or a quick-drying epoxy. The adhesive takes longer to cure, so if you use it, you'll have to weight down the board overnight while the adhesive sets up. After nailing the new board, patch and sand edges and nail holes so that it blends in perfectly.

Fractures

I see more cracks in factory-finished floors than in any other type of flooring. The finish on these boards is easily damaged by flooring nailers. Cracks also can form on the face of factory-finished and regular floorboards after installation. This damage is generally attributed to checks, or cracks, in the wood.

What to do

Factory-finished boards can be fixed with a manufacturer repair kit, which typically consists of wood filler, colored marker, and a bottle of finish. If you can't get a kit, proceed the same way as you would with regular flooring: Replace the board, or fill the crack with wood filler and apply a coat of finish over the entire floor so that colors, tones, and sheen match perfectly.

INSTALLATION ERRORS SHOW. The finish on the edge of this board was cracked by a flooring nailer that wasn't used correctly.

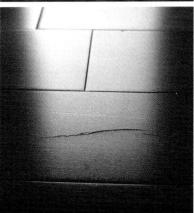

SMALL CRACKS CAN BE FILLED. A board with cracks in its face doesn't always need to be replaced. The board shown here can be repaired with a touch-up kit.

PET-STAINED FLOORS CAN BE SAVED. This floor can be fixed by brushing two-part wood bleach over the surface. The floor is neutralized after a couple of hours, then sanded and refinished when it's dry.

Stains

Stains can be traced to a variety of sources. Some spills only discolor a floor's finish, while others penetrate the wood itself. Pets are the most common culprit, but water can be just as damaging.

What to do

Stains built up on a floor finish can usually be removed with a wood-floor cleaner, but stains in the actual finish must be sanded out. The most difficult stains to deal with are those that penetrate into the wood fibers. I usually recommend replacing floorboards that have been deeply stained, especially by pet urine. But I have had success using two-part wood bleach (www.kleanstrip.com) to remove stains.

This treatment has some drawbacks, though. Bleach tends to break down wood fibers, increasing the wood's susceptibility to denting. Also, bleach isn't guaranteed to lift the stains from the wood, which means the floorboards might still need to be replaced. Finally, the entire floor should be bleached, not just one area. This results in a lot more work but helps to create a floor that is consistent in color and sheen.

Charles Peterson is a hardwood-flooring expert. He lives in Gales Ferry, Conn. Photos by the author, except for photo p. 58.

STANLEY

DRYWALL TECHNIQUES

JOINT
COMPOUND

JOINT
TAPE

TAPING KNIVES

UTILITY
KNIFE

DRYWALL SAW

SANDING
SPONGE

A DRYWALL TOOL KIT

BY MYRON R. FERGUSON

- Drywall panel or drywall patch to cover the repair (not shown)

- Measuring and cutting tools, including a tape measure, square, rasp, utility knife, and drywall saw

- Fastening tools, including screws, screwdriver, drill with screw-bit attachment; hammer

- Taping tools, including taping knives in various widths and a mud pan

- Joint compound and joint tape

- Sanding tools and materials, including a drywall sanding sponge and a hand sander with 180-grit or finer paper or sanding screen attached

- Dust mask made to filter small dust particles (and painter plastic to help contain the dust)

Myron R. Ferguson is a drywall contractor in Middle Grove, N.Y., and is the author of *Drywall* (The Taunton Press, 2012). Photos by Linda Ferguson.

SQUARE

TAPE MEASURE

RASP

DRYWALL SCREWS

DRILL

DUST MASK

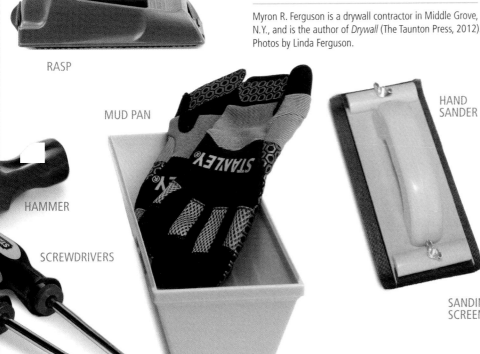

MUD PAN

HAMMER

SCREWDRIVERS

HAND SANDER

SANDING SCREENS

Hanging Drywall on Walls

BY MYRON R. FERGUSON ▪ I love working with drywall. That's not normally the sentiment you hear because, let's face it, hanging drywall is hard, dusty work. But there are ways to make it easier.

A good finished look starts with properly hung panels, which reduces the work of taping, mudding, and sanding. I try to use the biggest sheets possible to limit the number of seams I have to cover. If I'm working by myself, I can use 4-ft. by 12-ft. sheets. When I have a helper, I use 16-ft.-long sheets, if they are available at the supply store.

After I finish hanging the ceiling in a room, I hang the walls. I start where I can hang a full sheet without cutting it. Then I move to abutting walls where smaller pieces are required. This method limits the number of seams, which saves time and reduces waste. If my fastener misses a stud and finds nothing but air while I'm securing a sheet, I remove the fastener right then so there is no chance it will create a blemish on the finished wall.

Even if you are hanging just a few sheets, invest in a heavy-duty T-square to guide your cuts and a stiff-bladed keyhole saw to cut holes for outlet boxes and plumbing penetrations. Also, I use a fixed-blade utility knife that has a useful rasp built into the handle.

Myron R. Ferguson is a drywall contractor in Middle Grove, N.Y., and is the author of *Drywall* (The Taunton Press, 2012).

Hang from the top down

1 **MARK THE STUDS BEFORE YOU LIFT.** Position the drywall directly below where it will be installed. With a builder's crayon or pencil, mark each stud's location 7 in. down from the top edge.

2 **RAISE THE TOP SHEET INTO PLACE.** I use my left hand to lift and my right hand to stabilize. This way, my free hand can grab the cordless screwdriver when the sheet is in place.

3 **THE CRUCIAL MOMENT.** When working alone, lifting and fastening a sheet at the same time can be awkward. I hold up the sheet with my left hand and brace it with my shoulder while I drive the first screw.

TIP Avoid problems later. Most settling happens where the top plate meets the studs. To prevent cracks and fastener pops, I start my screw pattern 7 in. down from the top edge.

4 **SECURE FROM THE CENTER OUT.** I drive the bottom center screw first and then move out, first along the bottom edge, then up each stud at 16 in. on center. I use 1¼-in. fasteners for drywall thicknesses of ⅝ in. or less.

5 **LIFT THE LOWER PANEL INTO PLACE.** I lever the lower panel up against the upper panel's bottom edge with a drywall-lifting tool.

Use a T-square to cut a full sheet

1 **HOLD THE T-SQUARE IN PLACE WHILE YOU CUT.** Make the cut in the panel's good side. For safety, keep your top hand well off to the side and out of the path of the cutting blade. I use my foot to keep the bottom of the T-square in place. I start at the bottom and make the score in one motion.

2 **FINISH THE CUT.** I snap the board by lifting the center and pulling the board toward me. Then I insert my utility knife in the break and cut the paper on the back.

Cut the drywall in place to save time

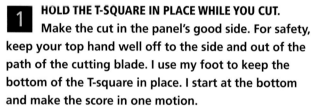

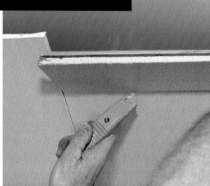

1 **SCORE THE BACK FIRST.** If there is scrap left in door and window openings, score the back of the sheet flush with the opening. Then break the scrap to the inside.

2 **WORK FROM THE SMOOTH SIDE TO COMPLETE THE CUT.** With the scrap pulled toward me to create a crease, I score the paper the full length. To ensure a clean edge, I push the scrap away from me to break the paper.

Taping Inside Corners

BY MYRON R. FERGUSON ▌ The average house has as much lineal footage of inside corners as it does flat seams. A good system for taping and mudding inside corners improves the look of every room and saves time.

Applying mud (drywall joint compound) and tape to an inside corner is difficult because it often involves blending three corners, like where the inside corner of a wall meets the ceiling (photo at left). For inside corners, I prefer to use paper tape instead of fiberglass-mesh tape because it is creased down the center, and is strong and easy to work with.

Before I tape inside corners, I tape and mud flat seams to ensure that the inside-corner tape laps over the flat-seam tape. Taping inside corners is done in three steps on three different days: one day for taping and two days for the finish coat.

After each coat dries, I use a pole sander with 150-grit paper to knock down bumps or rough spots. If you don't have a pole sander, you could use sandpaper wrapped around a flat wooden block. After the final coat, I use 150-grit (or finer) paper and sand more thoroughly.

Myron R. Ferguson is a drywall contractor in Middle Grove, N.Y., and is the author of *Drywall* (The Taunton Press, 2012).

Tape the flat joints before the corners

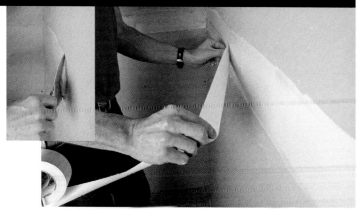

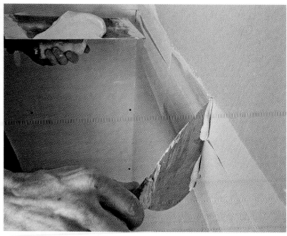

1 **SPREAD THE COMPOUND, AND PLACE THE TAPE.** Spread the joint compound at least ⅛ in. thick over the length of the joint. Starting in the corner, carefully place the tape on the surface of the compound over the joint. Press the tape into the compound.

2 **BED THE TAPE WITH A TAPING KNIFE.** Starting from the center, bed the tape by moving the knife against the joint with medium pressure, angled about 45°. To stop the tape from moving with the knife, press the corner of the hawk, or trowel, into the tape near the other end.

Bed the tape in the corners

1 **APPLY COMPOUND TO EACH SIDE OF THE CORNER.** Just as with the flat seams, don't skimp on the compound at this step. Compound ⅛ in. thick is about right.

2 **FOLD THE TAPE TO FIT IN THE CORNER.** All paper tape has a crease along the center to allow it to fold easily and fit in a corner. To place the tape, keep it pulled tight, pressing it into the corner every 24 in. instead of along the whole length.

TIP Tear the tape at an angle for a better fit at the ceiling. This allows the tape to fit tight without bunching.

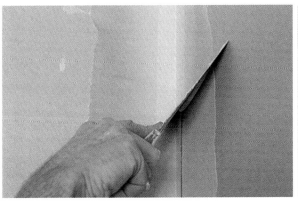

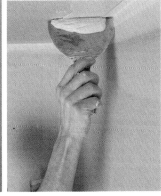

4 **APPLY TAPE TO THE CEILING LIKE THE CORNERS.** To apply more pressure, hold the knife at a steep angle. This enables the knife to press the tape tightly in the corner. After this pass, most of the compound is removed as the tape is embedded. The edge should be feathered right to the tape.

3 **BED TAPE FROM THE TOP.** At first, use light pressure with the knife to avoid pulling the tape away at the top. After the first foot of tape is set in the compound, apply more pressure.

Take two more days for the finish coat

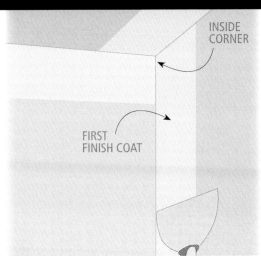

INSIDE CORNER

FIRST FINISH COAT

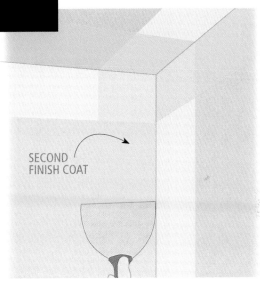

SECOND FINISH COAT

1 **ON THE SECOND DAY, FINISH ONE SIDE OF EVERY CORNER.** Apply the wet compound so that it does not overlap (shown in yellow above). The edge of the taping knife rides on the base coat of dry compound applied the day before. Keep the handle parallel to the adjoining wall to prevent the compound from loading up on that wall.

2 **ON THE THIRD DAY, FINISH THE CORNER'S OTHER SIDE.** While applying the other side of the finish coat (shown in blue), the edge of the taping knife rides on the adjoining dry coat of compound. If I'm careful not to let excess compound build up, I can achieve a nearly perfect inside corner that requires minimal sanding.

TIP During the finish coat, I hold the knife flatter to the wall to leave more compound over the tape. Feather the compound by pressing slightly harder on the outer edge of the taping knife. I feather the outside edge first, then smooth the inside corner with a second pass.

Finishing an Outside Corner

BY TOM O'BRIEN ▪ Finishing drywall can be a tricky art to master. If you've never finished drywall, the best place to practice is inside a closet. An outside corner is almost as good; if the corner bead is installed properly, its nose functions like a concrete form over which you screed the joint compound.

Corner bead is available in several materials, but the simplest to work with is the "tape-on" variety such as Beadex® (www.usg.com). This paper-faced metal bead installs without nails. You bed the paper in all-purpose joint compound. Many professionals say tape-on corner beads are less prone to stress cracks than traditional nail-on corner bead.

Adjoining corners and seams should be taped and allowed to dry before corner bead is applied.

Tom O'Brien is a carpenter in New Milford, Conn., and a former editor at *Fine Homebuilding.* Technical assistance by Darrell Lind of Woodbury Wall Systems in Woodbury, Conn.

Paper-faced bead goes on easily and stays put

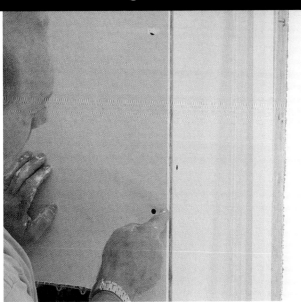

1 **START WITH A CORNER THAT'S STRAIGHT AND SECURE.** Check the framing for straightness before hanging the drywall, then carefully assemble the corner to avoid overhanging edges. Rule of thumb: Cut the first board flush with the edge of the corner stud; cut the second board to overlap halfway onto the first board. Secure the edges with screws placed no more than 12 in. apart.

2 **THE ADHESIVE COAT MUST BE THIN.** To enable the bead to seat tightly to the wall, add enough water to thin the compound to the consistency of thick pancake batter. Then spread a generous helping of compound in a 2-in.-wide swath on each side of the corner. Hold the knife almost flat, and apply slight pressure to ensure a uniform layer of compound.

3 **USE FINGER PRESSURE.** Bed the bead in the joint compound, and push it tight to the ceiling. Then run your thumb and finger along the paper edges, applying light pressure.

4 **WIPE THE EDGES GENTLY.** Use your taping knife to make sure that the nose stands proud of the wallboard on both sides of the bead. If it doesn't, use your fingertips to coax the bead to one side or the other. Once the bead is positioned correctly, hold the knife at a 45° angle and gently wipe both edges, using an index finger to flex the blade gently.

Two coats cover the corner: Coat one

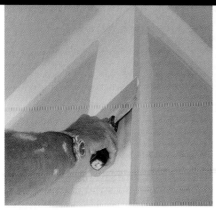

1 **SMOOTH THE FIRST COAT.**
Spread compound mixed with little or no water over one side of the corner, making sure that the nose of the bead is covered. Hold the knife at a shallow angle, and screed the compound between the bead and the inner wall surface. Make one long, smooth pass from the top and one from the bottom.

2 **THE SMOOTHING PROCESS.**
Feather the inside edge of the compound by holding the 8-in. taping knife at a 45° angle and applying pressure to the inner edge; the outer edge should not touch the mud.

3 **GETTING SMOOTHER.** Repeat step 1, but use your forefinger to apply slight inward pressure. After the final pass, the nose of bead should be as visible as the edge of a concrete form.

Coat two

1 **FILL GAPS WITH THE FINAL COAT.** Allow the first coat to dry, then sand lightly (100- to 150-grit paper) to knock off lap marks and other high spots. The final coat of joint compound should be slightly thinner than the previous one, yet thicker than the adhesive coat. Apply the compound using a 10-in. knife.

2 **SKIM, THEN SAND.** Hold the knife at a 45° angle, and apply slight, evenly distributed pressure. After this coat is dry, sand lightly using extrafine (150- to 220-grit) sandpaper, and you're done.

STANLEY

Repairing Drywall Damage

BY MYRON FERGUSON Your walls and ceilings are in need of a fresh coat of paint, so you get started by clearing out the area and removing pictures from the walls. That's when you invariably notice that the painted surfaces are a little banged up. Some repairs are simply necessitated by the demands of daily life in a busy household, where doorknobs may strike against walls, pets may scratch surfaces, and children may playfully bang toys against anything in their path. Other repairs may be necessary if the drywall develops cracks.

When done properly, repairs become a permanent and inconspicuous part of the wall or ceiling. Some repairs are simple and can be done with one or two thin coats of joint compound; others require additional support and at least three coats of compound.

Repairing Popped Fasteners

Popped nails and screws are one of the most common drywall problems. Fortunately, they're also among the easiest to repair. The problems occur when the drywall is not fastened tightly against the framing, when the framing lumber shrinks or twists, or when an object strikes the wall. With time or abuse, joint compound comes loose from the fastener and pops off, exposing the fastener head.

When repairing popped fasteners, keep the compound thin over the patched area and feather it out as wide as necessary so that it blends into the wall or ceiling. You'll need to apply three thin coats.

1 **SECURE THE DRYWALL. To** repair a popped nail or screw, place another screw 1½ in. away, and then remove or reset the popped fastener. Apply hand pressure to the panel next to the area as you set the new screw. (Note that this drill comes with a built-in light, which makes it easy to see the damaged area.)

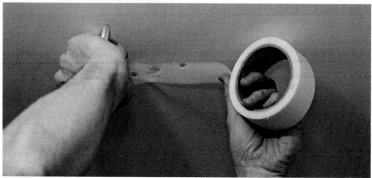

2 **COVER IT WITH COMPOUND. Most depressions left from** removing fasteners can be filled with compound alone, but if there is damage to the drywall surface, cover the heads with mesh tape before applying the compound.

Concealing Fastener Depressions

Areas around fastener heads where the joint compound is recessed below the surface of the panel are called fastener depressions. Depressions usually occur for one of two reasons: Either too little joint compound was applied during taping or the fastener was driven too deeply into the panel surface, damaging and weakening the panel's face paper and interior gypsum core. When sanded, the compound is removed from the indentation because the drywall pushes in as you sand over the loose fastener. The slight depression is visible at certain angles and under certain lighting conditions.

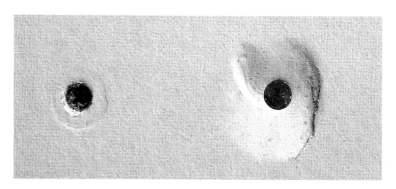

1 **FASTENERS POORLY SET. A properly set screw is set so that** the head is just below the surface of the drywall face (about 1 mm). Both the nail and the screw shown here are set improperly, creating the potential for a depressed area around the fastener, even after applying three coats of compound. (Resist the temptation to use a drywall nail instead of a drywall screw. Screws hold better and do less damage to the drywall core and paper face when installing and as a result are better for repairs.)

2 **TAPE AND MUD.** To repair a fastener depression, drive a drywall screw 1½ in. away, remove loose material, and then reset the original fastener. Prefilling with compound and using mesh tape may be necessary if damage is extensive.

Repairing Holes in Drywall

Holes in the drywall surface that result from long-term wear and tear range from small nail punctures to large gouges. The extent of the repair depends on the size of the hole. Nail holes, nicks, and small dents can simply be covered with compound; small holes require paper or mesh for reinforcement; and larger holes require the use of wood furring strips to support a drywall patch.

1 **PUSH IT IN.** Typically when a nail or picture hanger is pulled out, there is a slightly raised area around the small hole. Push it in with the handle of your taping knife.

2 **JUST A BIT OF COMPOUND.** Apply a small amount of joint compound using a 4-in. taping knife.

3 **SCRAPE IT OFF.** As you remove the compound, some will remain in the small hole and a thin film will be left on the painted surface surrounding the hole. Usually all that is needed is this one coat of compound. When dry, sand with a fine-grit sanding sponge.

Repairing small holes or dents

Whether from doorknobs or moving accidents, small holes or dents can be patched with a store-bought patch or with mesh tape.

1 CLEAN IT UP. Use a utility knife to remove any rough edges around the hole.

2 PATCH THE HOLE. To repair a small hole (less than 2 in. or so in diameter), cover it with a self-repair patch (shown here) or crisscross the hole with layers of mesh tape. Mesh tape should be pressed in slightly to create an indentation.

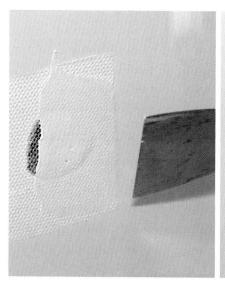

TIP The finish coat is a great time to start using a dust-control joint compound over a setting compound or premixed compound. Because most of the sanding is done after the final coat is dry, this will help reduce airborne dust.

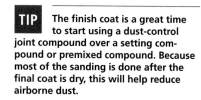

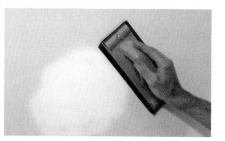

3 COVER IT WITH COMPOUND. Use a taping knife to force some of the compound through the mesh and into the hole.

4 SECOND COAT. Let the compound dry thoroughly before applying a second coat of compound. Feather out the compound, but be careful not to build up too much compound over the patched area. (A 6-in. taping knife works great for applying and smoothing out the second coat of compound on a repair this size.)

5 SAND AND REPEAT. When the second coat is dry, lightly sand with a hand sander (shown here) or a fine-grit sanding sponge, and then apply the finish coat of compound.

TAPING MATERIALS

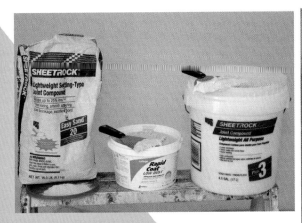

JOINT COMPOUND

There are three main options for joint compound: all-purpose ready-mixed compound, setting compound, and dust-control compound.

All-purpose ready-mixed joint compound is available in a variety of container sizes, so you purchase only what you need. It is premixed, but small amounts of water can be added to create the desired, workable consistency. All-purpose compound has to air-dry before the next coat can be applied. It can be applied as a finish coat over a setting compound, if desired; the advantage is that all-purpose is easier to sand than the setting type.

Setting compound comes in dry form in an 18-lb. bag and is mixed with water to the proper consistency; it sets up chemically, so multiple coats can be applied in a short period of time. Setting compound does not sand as easily and cannot be remixed when set up. It is available in a variety of setting times to meet your schedule.

A dust-control compound is essentially a ready-mixed compound with an additive that causes the dust particles to cling together and fall to the ground faster, so less dust travels throughout the building.

Note that whatever type of compound you use, you have to let it dry completely before applying primer and paint.

JOINT TAPE

Joint tape is used to reinforce seams and corners and to repair cracks and holes in drywall. Three types of tape are available: paper, fiberglass mesh, and fiber. Paper tape is the least expensive but is not the easiest to work with. It does work very well for repairing inside corners. Fiberglass mesh is self-adhesive and is applied over the repair before compound is applied, so it is very easy to work with on seams and for patches. Fiber tape is applied and finished just like paper tape, but it provides a thinner repair, which is important.

You can also buy various repair patches for drywall, including precut patches for small holes and precut kits for electrical outlets.

Repairing a small hole in the ceiling

For a small hole in a ceiling, it's best to use a self-adhesive patch that is reinforced with a thin piece of perforated aluminum. If you use the same kind of patch as for the wall repair on a ceiling, gravity will cause the compound to droop down before it has a chance to set or dry. Otherwise, the procedure is the same.

1 **CLEAN UP THE HOLE.** Use a drywall saw to clean up the edges of the hole.

2 **USE A PATCH.** To prevent the compound from dropping, use a metal-reinforced patch.

3 **COVER THE HOLE.** After removing the backing, cover the hole with the patch.

4 **FINISH UP.** Apply three coats of joint compound to the patch and then sand.

FEATHER IT OUT

The best way to conceal a repair is to keep "feathering out" the joint compound around the patch. The compound over the patch is applied with a 6-in. taping knife just thick enough to hide the tape, then the compound is feathered out to nothing. The compound is applied thicker than is needed and then mostly removed with a 10-in.- or 12-in.-wide knife as you feather out the edges.

The finish coat is usually just a thin skim coat of joint compound that fills where necessary and eliminates any tool marks and unfeathered edges.

Repairing large holes

If an area is badly damaged, cut it back until you reach solid drywall. To make the repair, cut a drywall patch and use it as a template to form the damaged area into a square (as shown below), rectangle, or circle. The patch has to be attached to something solid but not necessarily a piece of framing-size material. To provide a fastening surface for the patch, use a wooden furring strip (or strips) cut about 6 in. longer than the hole. Slide the furring into the hole, and secure it in place with drywall screws fastened through the drywall and into the furring. (For really large holes, you'll have to cut the drywall back to the nearest framing member and add cross framing, as when eliminating a window or door.) Fit the patch to the hole, and then screw the patch onto the furring. The repair is the same for walls and ceilings (shown here).

Myron R. Ferguson is a drywall contractor in Middle Grove, N.Y., and is the author of *Drywall* (The Taunton Press, 2012). Photos by Linda Ferguson.

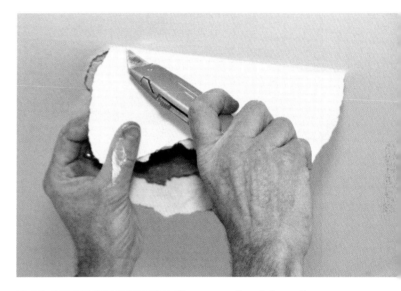

1 **ASSESS THE SITUATION. If you use the right techniques, repairing a large hole isn't that difficult.** First, cut away any loose material.

2 **POSITION A DRYWALL PATCH. Cut a drywall patch a little larger than the opening. Hold the patch over the damaged area, and trace its outline on the wall.** CONTINUED ON PAGE 82 ▶

CONTINUED FROM PAGE 81

3 **KEEP THE EDGES CLEAN.** Use a utility saw to cut out the damaged area.

4 **FUR OUT THE OPENING.** Slip furring strips into the squared-up hole, and attach them to the drywall with screws.

5 **ATTACH THE PATCH.** Position the drywall patch, and screw it to the furring. Cover the seams with mesh tape (typically mesh tape is used for repairs, but any of the three types of tape will work).

6 **ADD COMPOUND.** Larger holes require at least three coats of joint compound to be concealed properly. Be sure to feather the edges properly, and be careful not to build up the patched area too much.

7 **SMOOTH IT OUT.** A hand drywall sander attached to a vacuum (as shown here) is a great help for keeping dust down, but always wear a dust mask when sanding.

STANLEY

DOORS

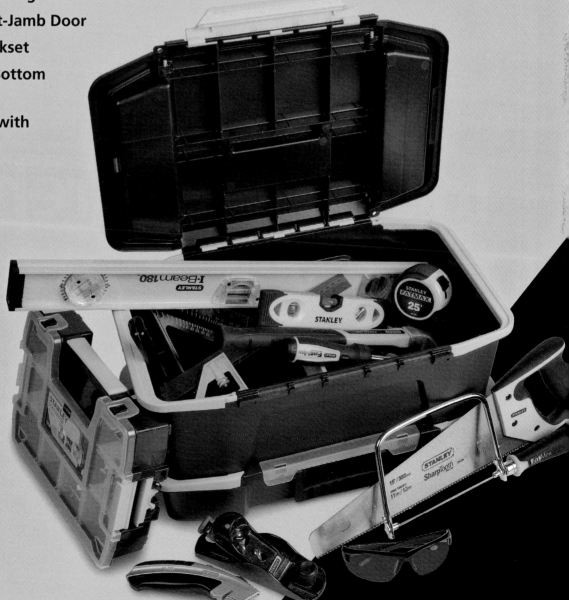

Installing a Prehung Exterior Door

BY ANDY ENGEL ▉ Installing a prehung exterior door is straight-forward. Assuming the wall is plumb and that the rough sill and opening are flashed, the first step is to check the rough sill for level. If it isn't level, set the door unit in place, and shim the low side until it is level. Add shims about every 6 in. for solid support. Remove the door unit without disturbing the shims, then bed the shims in window and door sealant.

Before placing the door in the opening permanently, squeeze several thick beads of sealant across the top of the sill flashing to keep out wind and rain.

Place the Door from the Outside

Most prehung doors are held closed for handling with some sort of bracket that fastens from the inside. If there's another way into the house, I leave this bracket in place for convenience. If this is the only easy way into the house, then I remove the bracket before proceeding so that I can get in the house through the new door.

Working from the outside, guide the unit into the opening, leading with the sill. When you feel the bottom of the door trim hit the side of the house, let the unit slide down until its sill rests on the rough sill. Push the top in until the trim is tight to the house.

Drive one 2½-in. deck screw through the door trim near the top hinge. This holds the door and allows adjustments while you continue working from the inside.

1 **CHECK FOR LEVEL. With the wall plumb and the opening flashed, check the sill for level. Use wood shims spaced every 6 in. as needed. Bed the shims in window and door sealant.**

2 **SET THE DOOR. After placing three continuous beads of sealant across the length of the rough sill, insert the door in the opening.**

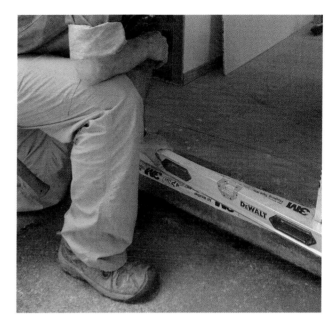

3 **DRIVE ONE SCREW. Install one screw through the door trim near the top hinge. This keeps the unit from toppling while still allowing it to be shimmed plumb.**

Shim the Door Plumb

You already shimmed the door sill level, so you can pretty much put away your level. Now it's a matter of shimming and fastening the unit so that the gaps between the door and the frame are uniform. Assuming the door is square, the unit will automatically be plumb when it's properly shimmed. Look first at the top of the door on the latch side. If the gap here is narrow, shimming the near bottom of the door frame at the latch side should open it up. If the gap is wide, shimming behind the lower hinge should close it.

Once you're happy with the gaps, shim behind each hinge, and replace the two innermost screws at each hinge with a 2½-in. screw driven into the stud. Moving to the latch side, shim behind the latch and about 12 in. above and below the latch to even out the gaps. Each set of shims should get two screws, one through the inner side and one through the outer side of the jamb.

After you've shimmed and screwed the frame, check the door's function. It should open and close without hitting the frame. If it hits the frame, back out the screws, adjust the shims, and rescrew. Once the door functions well, score the shims with a knife, and snap them off. Finally, go outside and use 2½-in. deck screws spaced about every 12 in. to screw the door trim to the house.

Senior *Fine Homebuilding* editor Andy Engel is a former carpenter who now spends weekends on unending home improvement.

1 **MIND THE GAP.** Check the space between the top of the door and the head jamb on the latch side so that you know where to shim first.

2 **SHIM THE HINGES.** To open the gap above the latch side, add shims behind the bottom hinge. To close the gap, reduce the shim thickness or shim the other side.

3 **FASTEN THE HINGES.** With each hinge shimmed so that the top gap is even, replace the two short inner screws with 2½-in. screws driven into the framing.

4 **ADJUST THE LATCH JAMB.** Once the hinge-side jamb is fastened, shim behind the latch-side jamb to even the gap.

SHIMMING

Start with two shims made from cedar shingles. Insert one thick end first, then insert the second so that the tapers oppose each other. Sometimes there's room for only one shim. At other times, the studs will have warped, and you'll need to insert shims with their tapers running in the same direction. Cut the shims as needed so that the fat end is the right thickness.

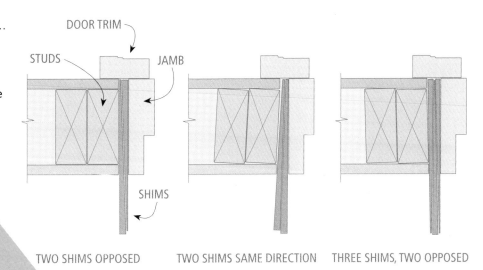

TWO SHIMS OPPOSED   TWO SHIMS SAME DIRECTION   THREE SHIMS, TWO OPPOSED

5 **FASTEN THE JAMBS.** Double-check the gap around the door, then drive two screws through each set of shims and into the framing.

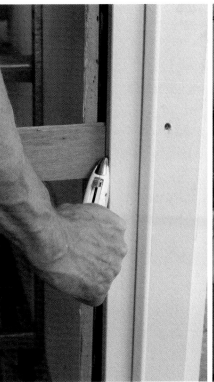

6 **SCORE AND SNAP.** After screwing through the shims, score them deeply with a sharp utility knife, then snap them off flush with the jamb.

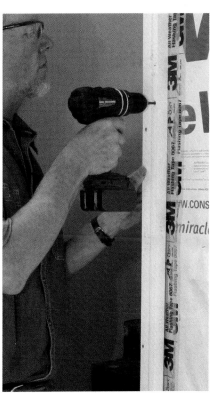

7 **SCREW THE DOOR TRIM.** After you've secured the jamb, screw the exterior trim to the framing. Use 2½-in. deck screws spaced about every 12 in.

Hanging a Split-Jamb Door

BY RICK ARNOLD Split-jamb doors are a lot like conventional pre-hung doors, but they have a two-piece jamb joined with a tongue and groove. The tongue-and-groove joint, which is hidden by the stop, allows both sides of the jamb to be cased at the millwork shop. Then the jamb can be separated when it's time to install the door.

Not only does the setup eliminate installing casing in the field, but it also gives you some wiggle room with regard to wall thickness. This quality makes split jambs great for old houses, which often have wavy plaster and odd-size studs. In addition, the millwork shop generally installs the casings and prepares the jambs for less than what I'd pay a competent finish carpenter to do the same work.

I've heard old-school carpenters deride split-jamb doors, claiming they can't be shimmed, but that's simply not the case. You just have to change your methods. I've never had a problem with any of the several hundred split-jamb doors I've installed over the years.

Rick Arnold is a *Fine Homebuilding* contributing editor.

1 CHECK FOR LEVEL. The first step is to check the floor under the jambs for level. A 32-in. spirit level and a graduated shim make it easy to see how much the floor is off.

2 TRIM THE JAMBS. If the floor is out of level, cut one of the jambs a corresponding amount shorter than the other jamb. If a tile or hardwood floor will be installed later, raise the jambs with scraps to match the floor's final height.

3 TRY THE FIT. Confirm that the hinge-side jamb can be made plumb in the opening. Then remove the door, and pull out the duplex nail or hardware holding the door to the jambs. Replace it with a single finish nail.

CONTINUED ON PAGE 90 ▷

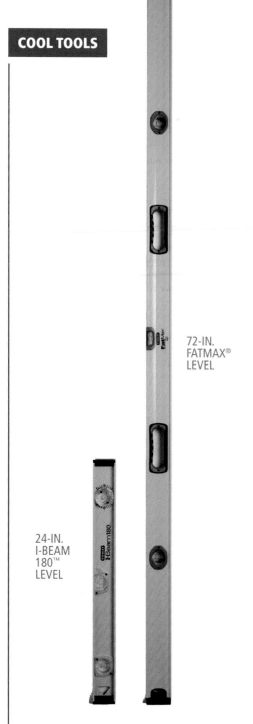

72-IN.
FATMAX®
LEVEL

24-IN.
I-BEAM
180™
LEVEL

The most important tools in the door hanger's kit are a pair of high-quality spirit levels to ensure a plumb door that doesn't open or close on its own.

CONTINUED FROM PAGE 89

4 **CASING HOLDS THE DOOR PLUMB.** Plumb the door with a level held along the casing leg, and drive 2½-in. finish nails through the casing into the jack studs and header.

5 **FREE THE DOOR.** Use a fine-tooth hacksaw blade held in a gloved hand to cut through the finish nail that holds the door closed. Go slowly so that you don't damage the jamb or stop.

6 **SHIMS STEADY THE JAMB.** Use 3-in.-wide shims (held vertically) to take up the space between the jamb and the rough opening. Tack the shims in place, but keep the nails away from the groove so that you can install the tongue side of the jamb later.

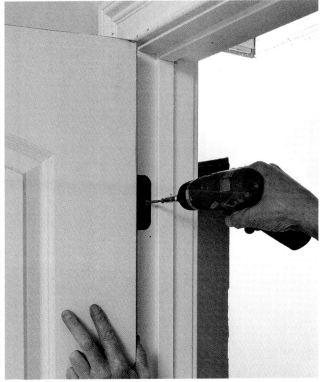

7 **JOIN THE JAMB.** Starting at the top, slip the remaining half of the split jamb onto the half already in place, and secure it by nailing through the stop and casing.

8 **SCREW THROUGH THE HINGES.** It's a good idea to swap one of the short screws in each hinge with one that goes into the framing. Plan for this; 2½-in. #9 wood screws in the correct finish are tough to find.

Installing a Lockset

BY TOM O'BRIEN ■ Unlike old-fashioned and complicated mortise locks, most of the locksets you see these days
are of the cylindrical variety and are fairly easy to install.
Basically, installation requires a large hole drilled through the
face of the door and a smaller hole drilled through the edge.
After the holes are drilled, the most difficult part of the job
is cutting the mortises for the strike and latch plates.

There are two keys to a successful installation: careful
layout and sharp tools. In addition to a tape measure, a
combination square, and a hammer, you'll need a scratch
awl, a 2⅛-in. hole saw, a $^{15}/_{16}$-in. spade bit, and a 1-in. chisel.
Assembling the lockset varies slightly from brand to brand,
so it's important to read the manufacturer's instructions.

Tom O'Brien is a carpenter in New Milford, Conn., and a former editor at *Fine Homebuilding*.

1 USE A COMBINATION SQUARE FOR LAYOUT. Most lockset packages include a paper template for locating the face and the edge bore. It's easier and more accurate to use a combination square, especially if you've got more than one lockset to install. Begin the job by wedging the door halfway open with a couple of shims under the bottom edge. Mark the face on both sides, 2⅜ in. from the leading edge of the door (2¾ in. for exterior doors) and typically 36 in. from the floor. The edge bore is marked at the center of the door, in line with the face marks.

2 PILOT HOLES PAVE THE WAY FOR THE BIG BITS. To make sure the holes for the cylinders start in the right place and don't wander, use a scratch awl to punch the precise starting points. Then drill pilot holes with a ⅛-in. bit in the edge and in both faces of the door.

3 DRILL THE FACE BORE FIRST. Holding the tool level and square to the door, drill halfway through one side with a 2⅛-in. hole saw. Then complete the bore from the other side of the door.

4 USE A NAIL TO MARK THE CENTER OF THE STRIKE-PLATE HOLE. Close the door and hold it tight to the stop, then push a 6d nail through the ⅛-in. pilot hole in the door edge until it pierces the door jamb; a pry bar provides leverage if necessary. Now drill holes for the latch and the strike using a ¹⁵⁄₁₆-in. spade bit. (A ⅞-in. bit is too small for most latch mechanisms, and the hole left by a 1-in. bit won't be covered completely by the latch plate.)

CONTINUED ON PAGE 94 ▶

COOL TOOLS

A JIG FOR FOOLPROOF HOLE ALIGNMENT

Carpenters who install door hardware for a living use commercial boring jigs that get the job done quickly and accurately. You can buy a light-duty version of the $250 jig for about $15. Made by Black & Decker®, this plastic jig clamps onto a door edge and aligns the face and edge holes automatically. Two hole saws (2⅛ in. and 1 in. dia.) and a common mandrel are included in the kit. The jig will handle both 2⅜-in. and 2¾-in. backsets.

5 **USE THE LATCH AS A TEMPLATE.** After drilling the edge bore, insert the latch mechanism and secure it with the screws provided, then trace around the edges with a sharp utility knife. Be especially careful when cutting vertically along the grain because the knife may wander. Some carpenters prefer to use a scratch awl to cut along the grain.

6 **CHISEL WITH CARE.** Hold a sharp chisel at about a 45° angle, and score the face of the mortise by tapping the chisel with a hammer; cut across the grain in increments of ⅛ in. Now carve away the waste, working toward the center. Check the fit of the latch plate; it should lie flush with the door surface. If you carve too deep, use cardboard to shim the plate flush with the edge of the door.

  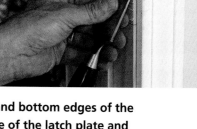

7 **ALIGN THE STRIKE WITH THE LATCH.** Close the door, and transfer the top and bottom edges of the latch plate to the door jamb. Now measure the space between the edge of the latch plate and the inside face of the door, and allow the same amount of space between the back of the strike plate and the doorstop. For a 1⅜-in. door (if the latch is centered properly), that space should be a heavy ⅛ in. The final task is to cut the strike mortise, following the same procedure used for the latch plate.

Trimming the Bottom of a Door

BY JOHN ROSS ▇ The necessity of trimming a door goes along with remodeling projects where the floor rises because of added carpeting, new tile, or extra layers of subflooring (or in my case, whenever my penchant for area rugs gets the best of me).

As someone who has remodeled other people's homes as well as my own, I have tackled this project over and over. To trim a door problem-free, I call on the same skills I use for other finish-carpentry projects, such as built-ins, wainscoting, and countertops.

Although you can use straightedge guides, special saws, and zero-clearance throat plates to cut finished work, I use a 4-ft. level clamped to the door and a thin-kerf blade in my circular saw for a task like this. I also use a utility knife to score the door and some masking tape to protect the surface of the door. Finally, I need a gauge block, which I usually make from a piece of thin plywood.

John Ross, a former *Fine Homebuilding* editor, is a freelance writer, editor, photographer, and video producer.

1 **MARK THE DOOR FOR THE CUT.** At the bottom of the door, I put tape on both the hinge side and the strike side (the side with no hinges). I place the rug against the closed door and mark both pieces of tape ¼ in. above the rug. Because this is an area rug and not wall-to-wall carpeting, I want the door just to clear the rug after it is trimmed.

2 **DRAW THE CUTLINE.** With the door set on saw-horses, I connect the two marks with tape, then use the level to draw a straight line between them.

3 **SCORE THE CUT TO PREVENT TEAROUT.** Clamped to the door, the level works well as a guide while I make several shallow passes with a utility knife to score the cutline. As an extra precaution, I tape and score the end of the door where the circular-saw blade will exit.

Use a gauge block to line up the cut

1 **MAKE A GAUGE BLOCK.** This scrap of wood is cut at the exact distance from the edge of the blade to the edge of the saw's baseplate.

2 **USE THE GAUGE BLOCK TO SET THE LEVEL BACK FROM THE CUTLINE.** The block should just cover the scored line. The level is secured to the door with two clamps.

3 **TAPE THE DOOR, NOT THE SAW.** To avoid marring the door, I put down two layers of tape next to the level. I tape the work because it's faster than taping the bottom of the saw and because it's easier to clean up.

5 **EASE THE EDGE.** To prevent the bottom of the door from splintering over time, I ease the edge using a small block plane. Some 80-grit sandpaper wrapped around a sanding block works just as well.

6 **THE PAYOFF.** The trimmed door clears the rug easily and doesn't look awkward.

4 **MAKE THE CUT.** I set the cutting depth so that the blade just cuts through the door (inset photo) and focus on the baseplate when making the cut. The baseplate edge stays in contact with the level while the bottom runs flat on the door. To prevent the blade guard from dragging on the door, I hold it retracted during the cut.

Casing a Door with Mitered Trim

BY TOM O'BRIEN ▬ There are almost as many ways to case a doorway (or a window frame) as there are carpenters. But in all cases, the keys to success are making sure that the corners of the jamb are perfectly square, that your miter saw is cutting accurately, and that you assemble the miters carefully (get them right and tight) before nailing the rest of the casing.

To permit the casing to lie flat, the jambs should be flush with, or slightly proud of, the wall surface. Plane the jambs if they're too far out; extend them with thin strips of wood if they're too far in. If the drywall is proud of the jamb by ⅛ in. or less, knock it back with a hammer.

If you have only one or two doors to case, a 16-oz. hammer and a nailset will get the job done just as quickly as an air nailer.

Tom O'Brien is a carpenter in New Milford, Conn., and a former editor at *Fine Homebuilding*. Technical assistance by Tim Carney of Carney Home Enterprises in New Milford, Conn.

Prep the jambs and precut the miters

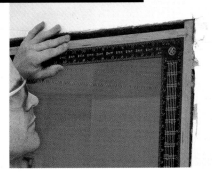

1 **LAY OUT FOR THE REVEAL.** Use a combination square and a sharp pencil to scribe the reveal, the distance (typically 3/16 in.) between the edge of the jamb and the casing. There's no need for a continuous line; simply scribe a dash every foot or two, making sure that the dashes meet in the corners.

2 **START SQUARE TO STAY SQUARE.** Check the jambs for square, and shim them if they're not. Otherwise, you may have to custom-fit the miter. Also, check the miter saw to verify that the blade is square to the table and to the fence; if so, the miter settings should be dead on. Refer to the owner's manual if adjustments are necessary.

3 **CUT MITERS IN ADVANCE.** Miter the side casings and one end of the head casing. Leave enough extra to cut these pieces to length later.

Mark in place, then install with glue and finishing nails

1 **INSTALL HEAD CASING FIRST.** Align the mitered end of the head casing with the corner of the reveal, and mark the point where the far end meets the reveal. After cutting the miter, position the casing carefully, and tack it to the jamb with 4d nails; leave nail heads about ¼ in. proud in case adjustments are necessary.

2 **MARK THE SIDES UPSIDE DOWN.** Flip the side casing so that the mitered end touches the floor, and mark the point where the bottom intersects the top of the head casing. Make a square cut, and you're ready to install the side casing. A word of warning: If the finished floor is severely uneven, you may need to use scribes or a contour gauge to transfer the floor's profile to the casing before making the cut. CONTINUED ON PAGE 100

A JIG FOR MEASURING AND MARKING CASING

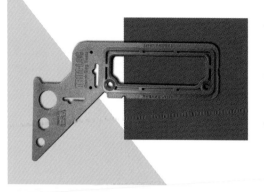

The Trim-Loc® casement-installation tool (www.benchdog.com) is essentially a triangle square that has been designed for casing. Its compact shape fits easily in a nail pouch. Like a Speed® Square, the tool has legs for marking 45° and 90° angles, but it includes extra features such as a gauge for scribing a ³⁄₁₆-in. reveal. It also can be fastened to a workbench for use as a jig to transfer measurements accurately from the inside of a miter.

CONTINUED FROM PAGE 99

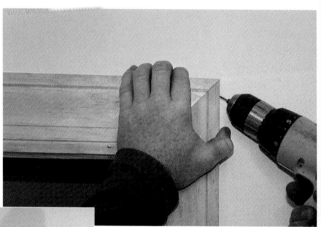

3 **GLUE AND NAIL THE CORNER.** Apply a generous amount of carpenter's glue to the end grain. Then carefully align the miter joint, and tack the side casing to the jamb with two or three 4d nails. Place the first nail about 1 in. from the corner. Blunt the point of this nail with a hammer to minimize the risk of splitting wood. Secure the outside corner of the miter by driving a 4d nail up through the edge of the side casing into the head casing; drill a pilot hole for the nail to prevent knocking the whole thing out of whack.

4 **EYEBALL THE SPACING.** After the miters are fixed, the casing is nailed home. Use 4d nails to fasten the casing to the jambs; 6d or 8d nails are needed to secure the casing to the framing. Nails should be placed an inch or two from each end and the same distance from the hinges. Otherwise, space the nails 8 in. to 16 in. apart. Leave all the heads slightly proud of the surface, then use a nailset to drive them about ⅛ in. below the surface.

STANLEY®

WINDOWS

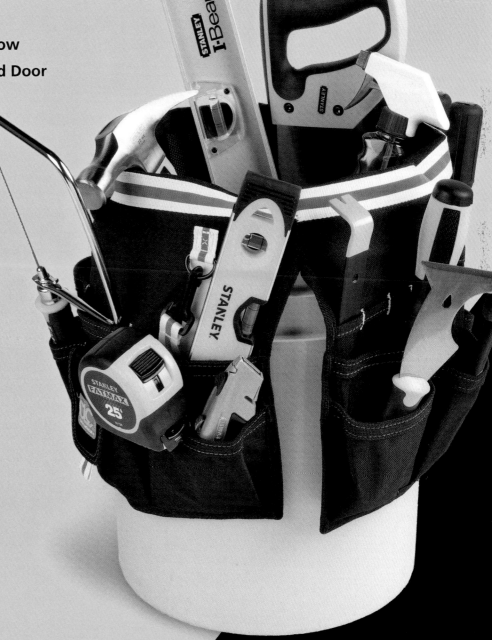

Replacing a Wood Window

BY SCOTT GRICE Aesthetically, old windows have charm to spare. Functionally, they aren't so charming. The first phase of replacing a window includes measuring for the new window, removing the old one, and prepping the opening. For this job, I chose a wood window to match the windows in the house and ordered it without stock trim or brick mold so that I could match the trim.

I sized the new window to fit without having to cut back or patch the existing siding. (I replaced one piece of siding above the window in phase 2.) The rough opening, however, needed blocking to close the sash-weight space that old windows have and new windows don't. For this, I use 2x lumber that matches the existing framing.

There's nothing charming about having a piece of plywood covering a hole in the house while I wait for the new window to arrive, so I always make sure the new window is what I ordered before I remove the old unit.

Next, I start on phase 2, which entails setting the new window, weatherizing it, and applying the interior and exterior trim.

Remodeling, repairing, and upgrading older homes can present challenging circumstances. Rough openings are often out of square or out of plane. Weatherizing is like trying to make a Wiffle® ball airtight, and plumb and straight are often less important than parallel and perpendicular. In other words, the success of a project like the window replacement shown here often lies in the compromises.

For example, if this had been a new home or a remodel that entailed stripping the siding, I would have lapped housewrap into the rough opening first. I also may have used a flanged window, which would have allowed me to lay flexible flashings over the housewrap and onto the window.

Scott Grice, a frequent contributor to *Fine Homebuilding,* is a carpenter in Portland, Ore., and also holds a degree in philosophy.

Measure for the new window

STOOL

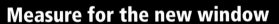

1 **MEASURE THE EXISTING SASH.** To size the new window, measure the distance between the inside of the window tracks for both width and height. Add 1½ in. (¾ in. for each jamb) to the width and ¾ in. plus the thickness of the stool to the height. This will give you the outside dimension to use for ordering a new window.

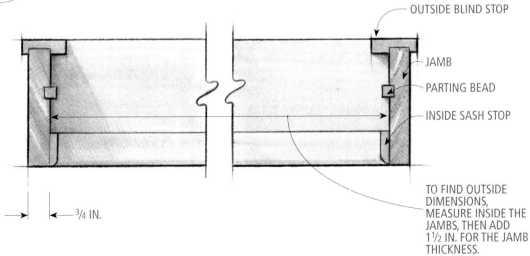

OUTSIDE BLIND STOP

JAMB

PARTING BEAD

INSIDE SASH STOP

¾ IN.

TO FIND OUTSIDE DIMENSIONS, MEASURE INSIDE THE JAMBS, THEN ADD 1½ IN. FOR THE JAMB THICKNESS.

READY-MADE PAN FLASHING

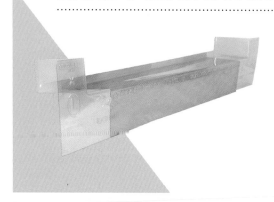

Flashing tape isn't the most fun material to work with. Depending on the kind you get, it will either stick to everything tenaciously or nothing at all. Whatever the case, it can be frustrating. For those who don't want to fashion a sill pan from scratch, there are manufactured pan-flashing systems available, such as the Dow® Weathermate™ Sill Pan, shown here (www.dow.com). This can be an economical option if you don't have a lot of windows to install. They come in various sizes to fit an opening's width.

John Ross, a former *Fine Homebuilding* editor, is a freelance writer, editor, photographer, and video producer.

Remove the old window

1 **SASH FIRST.** It's safer and easier to remove the window frame with the operational sash taken out. With a pry bar, remove the inside sash stops. Cut the sash-weight cords, and let the weights fall into the cavity. With the stops and cord removed, the lower sash should easily lift out.

2 **TRIM SECOND.** To ensure that the house paint remains intact, score the seam between the trim and siding before prying the trim loose. Windows made before the mid-1950s have a cavity behind the trim to house the sash weights.

3 **WEIGHTS, THEN WINDOW.** After pulling out the loose sash weights, remove any fasteners holding the window in place, and lift the entire window frame from the opening in one piece.

Prep the rough opening

1 **ADD BLOCKING.** Once the old window frame is removed, clear debris and errant nails. Use 2x lumber and spacers to block in the sash-weight cavity and to create the appropriately sized rough opening for the new window.

2 **FUR OUT THE BLOCKING.** The front face of the new rough opening should be flush with the sheathing. In this case, the author was able to use the old window trim, ripped to width, as furring.

Install flexible flashing

1 **FLASH THE SILL FIRST.** Use self-adhesive flexible flashing to create a waterproof sill pan. First, spread the flashing across the rough opening (photo above). Then cut down along the inside edge of the opening, and lay the flashing across the sill. To seal the corners, run another 8-in. to 10-in. piece of flashing down the side of the opening, lapping it over the top of the sill pan and down the front (inset photo).

2 **FLASH THE SIDES AND TOP.** Apply 4-in.- to 6-in.- wide flashing to the sides first, then the top. (The author used a wider brand for the sill pan, thus the different colors.) The flashing should abut the siding, but don't worry about getting the flashing behind the siding because that could create more leaks than it would prevent.

Set and secure the window

1 SET THE WINDOW IN THE OPENING. Stop blocks help to align the window flush with the sheathing. Insert shims between the side of the window and the framing at the top and bottom to hold the window in place temporarily.

2 CENTER THE WINDOW TO THE SIDING. Adjust the shims to center the window. Use a level to ensure that the window is plumb, then cross-measure and square the window to within ⅛ in. This should closely match the center of the rough opening. If the existing edge of the siding is out of plumb by more than ¼ in., you may have to taper the trim or cut the siding to make up the difference.

3 SECURE THE WINDOW. Shim the window every 2 ft. or so along the sides (but do not shim or use fasteners above the window), and drive trim-head screws through the jamb into the framing at the shim locations. With a level, ensure that the window frame is straight. If necessary, back out the screws, and adjust them. As a final check, make sure that the sashes move up and down smoothly.

Apply exterior trim

1 INSTALL THE HEAD CASING. For wooden windows without a plastic flange, the trim helps secure the window in place and acts as a weather barrier. Back-caulk all exterior trim (applying a fat bead of caulk around the perimeter of the trim's back face). Use 15-ga. nails to attach the trim to the window jamb and to the framing. Once the head trim is installed, apply metal cap flashing. If necessary, replace the one piece of siding above the window to aid in the cap-flashing installation.

2 INSTALL THE SIDE CASING. Size the window trim to leave a ¼-in. to ⅜-in. jamb reveal and to abut tightly against the existing siding. As with the head casing, prime the side casing on all sides and back-caulk it during installation. Bevel the bottom of the casing leg if it rests on a sloped windowsill. Last, keep a uniform nailing pattern for an ordered and pleasing final look.

IT REALLY IS GREAT STUFF

Back in the dark ages, it was acceptable to stuff fiberglass insulation between a window jamb and the surrounding framing members and call that weatherization. Not anymore. Builders have learned that without air-sealing, fiberglass insulation is all but useless.

Today, builders use expanding polyurethane foam to seal gaps around windows and doors. With only a handful of brands and fewer types of foam to choose from, it's important to use the right one.

Products labeled "insulating" or "expanding" foam sealant can expand considerably and powerfully. This is great when you need to seal a large gap, but it can distort a jamb to the point that the window sash or door will bind. For the small gaps found between jambs and rough openings, use a minimally expanding product labeled for windows and doors.

Cans of expanding foam can seem pricey, but they are worth the expense. A note of caution: The foam is difficult to clean up, so protect all surfaces before you begin, and have a can of mineral spirits on hand. —JOHN ROSS

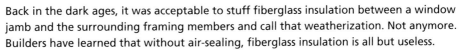

Insulate and trim the interior

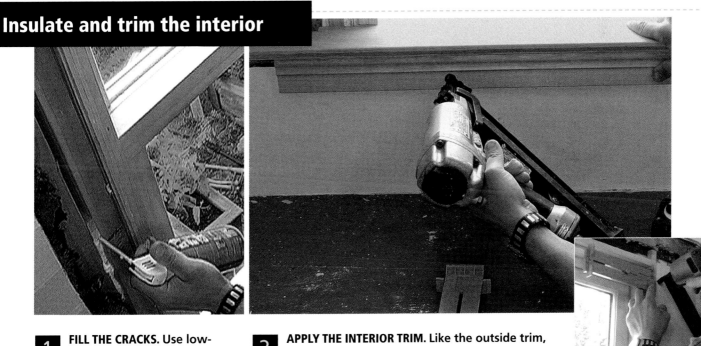

1 FILL THE CRACKS. Use low-volume expanding foam to fill the void between the window jamb and the framing.

2 APPLY THE INTERIOR TRIM. Like the outside trim, the interior trim helps to secure the window in place. Use 18-ga. fasteners for the trim-to-window connection and 16-ga. fasteners for the trim-to-framing connection. As shown in the inset photo, you can use a reveal gauge to maintain a consistent reveal between the edge of the trim and the edge of the window jamb.

Air-Sealing Windows and Doors

BY MIKE SLOGGATT To the uninitiated, it might appear that once a new door or window is in the rough opening and the exterior is flashed, the installation is done and it's time to install the trim or move on to something else.

1 **START AT THE TOP.** With the foam-gun nozzle inserted between the door or window frame and the rough opening, close the gap with a single bead of foam. Leave the rest of the space between the frame and the rough framing open so that infiltrated water can drain. Start as far away as you can reach, and work toward yourself.

Stopping the installation there, however, leaves out a very important step: air-sealing the interior. Air leaks around doors and windows not only significantly increase energy losses and make a house less comfortable, but the resulting cold spots inside the wall also can create condensing surfaces that wet insulation and damage framing and finishes.

Modern spray foam makes air-sealing around windows and doors fast and easy. The secret is to use a low-pressure, low-expansion, closed-cell foam designed for windows and doors, and to apply it with a pro-style foam gun.

Don't use expanding foams (often marketed as crack-and-gap fillers), which can exert enough pressure to distort frames and hinder door and window operation. Also, before air-sealing, make sure that the door or window works perfectly because the foam makes later adjustments extremely difficult.

Polyurethane foam sticks tenaciously to just about anything it touches, so keep it away from finished surfaces and home furnishings. Also, wipe away messes on hard surfaces as soon as they occur.

You can clean up uncured foam on soft materials with acetone or aerosol cleaners made by foam manufacturers, but when the foam is sitting on the surface, it's generally easier and less damaging to let it dry and then to cut, pick, or scrape it off.

Mike Sloggatt is a remodeling contractor in Levittown, N.Y.

GO WITH A PRO

A pro-style foam gun is vastly superior to the plastic straw that comes with the cans of foam sold at home centers. The tool features a small nozzle that can fit in tight spots and an adjustable trigger for improved control. The cans of foam it accepts are also a better value than straw-dispensed cans, yielding more foam at a lower cost with almost no waste.

TIP A light coat of cooking spray on the gun's nozzle prevents dispensed foam from sticking to the gun, resulting in a neater job and easier cleanup.

2 **SEAL THE SIDES.** Once the top is done, seal the sides by working from the top down and using the edge of the jamb to guide the nozzle for a neater job. To make cleanup easier, periodically wipe the gun's nozzle of accumulated foam with a rag or paper towel before it dries.

3 **SEAL MANUFACTURED SILL PANS WITH CAULK.** The tiny gap between window and door frames and manufactured sill pans is better sealed with window-and-door caulk rather than foam. Seal only the top edge of the pan's back dam so that water can drain from beneath. Painter's tape ensures a tidy job.

CONTINUED ON PAGE 110 ▶

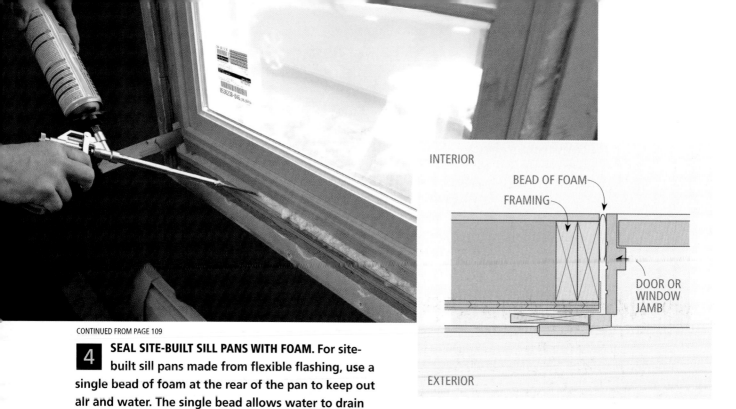

INTERIOR

BEAD OF FOAM

FRAMING

DOOR OR WINDOW JAMB

EXTERIOR

CONTINUED FROM PAGE 109

4 **SEAL SITE-BUILT SILL PANS WITH FOAM.** For site-built sill pans made from flexible flashing, use a single bead of foam at the rear of the pan to keep out air and water. The single bead allows water to drain while stopping air movement.

TIP Consider extension tips. Some guns accept small-diameter metal extension tips that make it easier to slip the nozzle into the space between the jamb and the rough opening. Other guns have a barbed tip that accepts flexible plastic nozzles. Both styles work well.

5 **TRIM THE FOAM.** Once the foam has had a chance to set up thoroughly, usually after about an hour, trim the foam flush with the opening using a reciprocating-saw blade or a keyhole saw.

6 **COVER THE SHIMS.** If you haven't already trimmed the shims used to level the unit, cut them off so that they're flush or below the framing. Cover the ends of the shims with foam, and fill any remaining gaps in the foam previously installed.

7 **KEEP A CAN OF FOAM ON THE GUN.** Polyurethane foam cures with exposure to humidity, so make sure the gun is airtight by keeping a can of foam on it at all times, even if the can is empty. If you won't be using the gun for several weeks, replace the can of foam with a can of cleaner. Run the cleaner through the gun until the spray is clear.

STANLEY.

ELECTRICAL REPAIRS

AN ELECTRICAL TOOL KIT

BY BRIAN WALO

I could easily blow everything I earn as a professional electrician in a single afternoon buying fancy tools that I might use some day for some thing. When I check back into reality, though, I have to admit that it's still the most basic electrical tools that I always reach for. Besides, if I'm going to remain efficient, I have to choose the tools that provide the most bang for my buck and leave my electrical-tool bucket light enough to move around easily.

Also, some tools in my kit (not shown here) are basic items that apply to all sorts of remodeling tasks. I choose these tools based on their use in electrical applications, though. For instance, rather than a heavy 18v drill/driver, I carry an ultracompact model with long-lasting Li-ion batteries to save space without sacrificing run-time. This kit won't get you in and out of complex jobs, but for most of the electrical work around your house, it will be your new best friend.

TESTERS

1. Analog/digital multimeter This is my first line of defense against electrical shock and an excellent diagnostic tool. I can double-check that I shut off the right breaker by using the multimeter's AC-voltage function; I also can figure out which cable runs to a light from a particular switch box. I use a clamp-on multimeter because it limits my exposure to bare conductors when I need to take an amperage reading on live equipment.

2. Noncontact voltage detector This little tool has a big gee-whiz factor because you can check for voltage without touch-

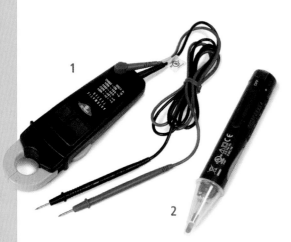

ing bare wires. However, different types of wire insulation and other nearby conductors can interfere with the electrical field, so this tool can be less than 100% reliable. Read the safety manual, and understand the tool's limitations. This is not an empty safety reminder, either. I have two pairs of wire strippers with arc holes that resulted from relying on this device before cutting a cable.

3. GFCI-outlet tester This little tester is the quickest way to check a GFCI outlet for proper wiring and fault protection. It's also a fast way to figure out which breaker powers a given circuit.

DRIVERS

1. Phillips head #2 and #3 Old electrical screws typically were slotted for a flathead screwdriver; modern versions now also accept Phillips-head drivers. The #2 and #3 are the two must-have sizes for electrical work.

2. Flathead ³/₁₆ in. and ¼ in. I hate slotted screws, but they are common. For electrical cover plates, ³/₁₆ in. is the standard; the ¼-in. size comes in handy as a "beater" for breaking the spot welds on the knockouts of a metal electrical box.

3. Nut driver Most grounding screws for metal workboxes have a ⁵/₁₆-in. hex head. I find a ⁵/₁₆-in. nut driver to be the quickest means of tightening them.

4. Robertson #1 and #2 These square-drive screwdrivers are my favorite tool, and no one else I know uses them. Most new devices (receptacles, switches, etc.) feature screws that can be driven with Phillips, flathead, or Robertson (square) screwdrivers, the latter of which provides the most positive grip.

PLIERS

1. Side-cutting (aka lineman's) Whether I'm pulling and clipping cable, or twisting wires together, these pliers are the most crucial and frequently used tool I own.

2. Crimpers Find a pair that is long and slender so that you can crimp together ground wires deep inside an electrical box. I also like crimpers with a cutter built in to the nose for slicing through the copper crimping sleeve to separate old ground-wire connections.

3. Strippers Even the most basic wire strippers are adequate, but I look for a set that has a long nose for reaching into tight

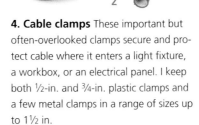

spots and serrated jaws to help me pull wire through the back of electrical boxes.

4. End cut This tool will be your first choice for pulling out cable staples from a stud or yanking nails from electrical boxes or can lights. A good set has sharp tangs and a solid bite for clipping through nails and staples.

5. Needle nose The fairly precise control of these pliers is great for getting me out of jams—for instance, if I drop a screw in the back of a crowded electrical box or need to pull some cable through a hole in a stud or plate.

MATERIALS

1. Electrical tape Black tape is the standard, but I also carry rolls of white and green so that I can mark grounded and ungrounded conductors for easy identification.

2. Wire nuts If I had to pick one wire nut to cover the bulk of my day-to-day work, it would be 3M Performance Plus Tan/Red wire connectors. These nuts handle from #22 to #8 AWG (American wire gauge) wires, depending on the number of conductors.

3. Crimping sleeves and bonding screws Most, if not all, codes require grounding conductors to be joined together, especially where they enter a metallic workbox. A jar of various sizes of copper crimping sleeves and #10 green ground screws is a must-have.

4. Cable clamps These important but often-overlooked clamps secure and protect cable where it enters a light fixture, a workbox, or an electrical panel. I keep both ½-in. and ¾-in. plastic clamps and a few metal clamps in a range of sizes up to 1½ in.

5. Staples Most of the cable I install is #12 and #14 AWG, so I keep lots of insulated staples in these two sizes.

6. Screws When I have to install workbox extensions in a kitchen backsplash or I lose a fastener from a fixture, #6x32 and #8x32 screws save the day. I buy them long and cut them to length with my strippers.

AREN'T YOU FORGETTING...

1. Diagonal cutters? Often called "diags" or "dykes," these cutters are a common electrical tool. I typically use strippers or lineman's pliers for most tasks suited to dykes, so I really can't justify their placement in my essentials kit.

2. Multibit screwdriver? I don't actually own a multibit screwdriver, but I am guilty of borrowing them. If you don't have room for individual drivers of all shapes and sizes, a good combo driver is a fine choice but only if it's fully equipped. Don't keep carrying it around if half the bits are lost.

3. Fish tape? Running new wires through existing walls is a frequent task during remodeling projects. But I don't own a single fish tape or anything else designed for snaking wires. Instead, I carry 10 ft. of ½-in. PEX tubing. The tubing is rigid enough to slide through walls. I use it as a channel to get the cable where I want it, and then I pull out the PEX like I'm taking off a sock.

Brian Walo is an electrician in Mount Pleasant, S.C.

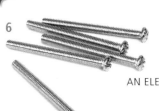

Working Safely Around Electricity

BY CLIFFORD A. POPEJOY ▓ Doing your own electrical work is satisfying, gets the job done on your schedule, and saves you money. That said, working with household current puts you within reach of a lethal dose of electricity. That's why it's essential to do electrical work with the power off. According to a government report, about one person dies every week in a construction-related electrical accident. To verify that power is off, use a voltage tester. Several different testers are shown here.

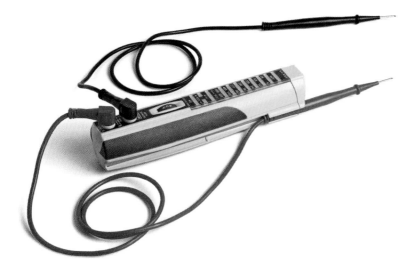

For basic wiring tests, I like a simple, rugged tester such as the Ideal Vol-Con® Elite with shaker, shown at left (www.idealindustries. com). This tester vibrates when voltage is present, helpful even if I can't see the indicator lights. The Vol-Con Elite also has a noncontact tester that identifies live wires through insulation as well as a similar feature in which one probe discerns voltage in a single wire. I run into this frequently with knob-and-tube wiring.

When shopping for a voltage tester, buy quality. Look for an Underwriters Laboratories (UL) listing and a Category III rating, which means the tester won't melt down in the event of unexpected high voltage.

Clifford A. Popejoy is a licensed electrical contractor in Sacramento, Calif. Photos by the author, except for the top photos on the facing page and all photos on page 116.

TWO MORE DEPENDABLE TESTERS

The Fluke T5-600 (en-us.fluke.com) is a rugged voltage tester with all the features of a multimeter. It checks for continuity, and it reads voltage, amperage (a built-in fork reads current through the wire's insulation), and ohms. The Greenlee GT-11 Non-Contact Voltage Detector (www.greenlee.com) does quick checks for voltage through insulation. I use it to double-check volt-meter results before touching a bare wire.

FLUKE T5-600

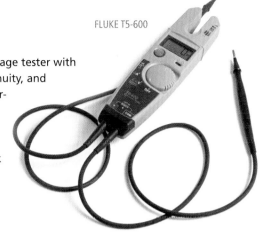

GREENLEE GT-11

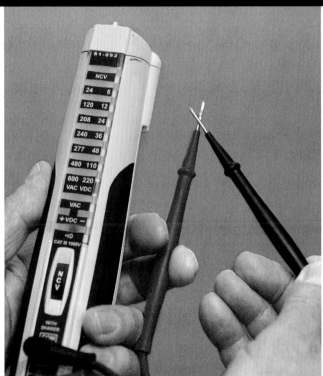

Test loose wires with clips and caps

CHECK THE TESTER'S BODY, PROBES, AND WIRES FOR SIGNS OF WEAR. Turn on the tester, cross the probe tips, and shake the wires. The continuity light and buzzer should remain on. Last, check the tester on a known live circuit. If the tester isn't reliable, have it repaired or replace it.

DON'T HOLD PROBES ON LOOSE WIRES. Put a wire nut on the end of loose wires, and place the probe in the wire nut. Make sure wires are free of oxidation or crud to avoid incorrect readings.

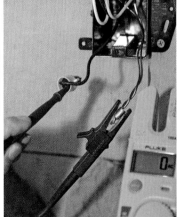

USE AN ALLIGATOR CLIP ON THE NEUTRAL if you're checking voltage at several points, such as several hot wires to a neutral wire. This way, you can focus on the probe checking the hot wires.

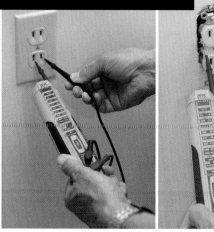
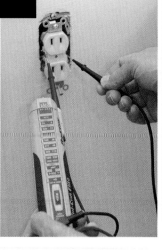

CHECK FOR VOLTAGE. Unlike plug-in testers, probe testers verify voltage both within the slots of a receptacle and on side terminals. Place one probe on the neutral (or taller) slot first, then on the hot (shorter) slot. The tester should read 120v. Remove the probes in reverse order. Hold the probes back from the tip to avoid shock if a wire moves or your hand slips.

QUICK RECEPTACLE TEST. Check for obvious problems in a grounding (three-hole) outlet by placing the tester's probe in the two vertical slots. The tester should read 120v. A properly grounded receptacle should read 120v with one probe in the shorter, hot slot and one probe in the grounding hole, as shown. If these tests show no voltage, either power is not present or the neutral (or ground) wire is interrupted or absent.

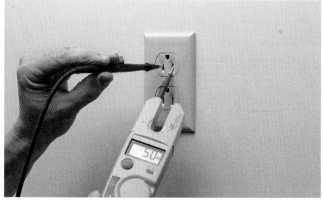

POLARITY IS IMPORTANT. Tools, appliances, and fixtures are designed so that power comes in on one of the two wires in a power cord. Reversing this arrangement, called polarity, can result in harmful shocks. Check for correct polarity by placing one probe in the grounding hole and the other in the shorter, hot slot. The meter should read 120v. Remove the probe from the hot slot and place it in the neutral slot. The meter should read 0v and also show continuity. Reversed readings mean that the polarity of the receptacle is reversed.

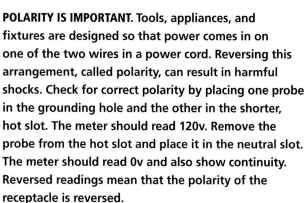

DEALING WITH PHANTOM VOLTAGE. Here's the situation: You think that you've turned off the correct circuit breaker, but a hot-to-neutral receptacle test reads 50v. If the circuit is de-energized, it should read 0v. Or, if the circuit is mislabeled and is still on, the tester should read 120v. You may be getting a false-positive reading, known as phantom voltage. Phantom voltage is caused by a live cable that induces a harmless voltage on a parallel de-energized cable. The simplest way to get a true reading is to use a solenoid-type tester, such as the Ideal Vol-Con Elite.

4 Worry-Free Wiring Repairs

BY BRIAN WALO When I tell people that I'm an electrician, they always say the same thing: "I'll do anything but electrical work." It's true that working with electricity can be dangerous, but so can working with power tools or even a kitchen knife. The keys to being safe are following a few basic rules and knowing something about the fundamentals of electricity. Whether you're replacing a broken switch or outlet or updating a fixture, the procedure is basically the same—provided you follow the rules and pay attention to detail.

It also helps to know a little about electricity itself. The fundamental electrical concept that guides my work is that of the circuit. At its most basic level, electricity flows in a circle. A battery is a good example. Batteries have a positive and a negative terminal—an "in" and an "out" if it's easier to think of it that way. Looping a wire from one terminal through a lightbulb and back to the other terminal completes the circle and lights the bulb. Transfer that idea of a circular path to your home wiring, and you'll have a much easier time making sense of any repairs you need to make.

Home Electricity at a Glance

The conductor (wire) that supplies power to a switch, socket, or lamp is called the "hot" or "in" side of the power supply. It's typically a black or red wire and is a constant power source coming from the electrical panel to outlets, switches, and lights.

A hot conductor must be paired with a neutral conductor (wire) to make a complete circuit. Neutral conductors are generally white or gray and constitute the "out" portion of the circle. If you look at an unplugged lamp, you can trace the path of electricity from the small end of the plug (hot/in), through the switch, through the bulb, and back to the large end of the plug (neutral/out). What this means is that every circuit in your house is really just a circle of energy.

Most residential electrical systems installed in the past 50 years also include a grounding conductor or ground wire. This additional wire helps to safeguard against electric shock or fire in the event of an electrical fault (any unintended discharge of energy, as when a loose wire contacts metal) by channeling that excess energy back to the ground and/or panel, where it should trip the breaker or blow the fuse. Grounding wires are generally bare or sheathed in green insulation and are not intended to carry electricity unless there is a malfunction. Never use a grounding wire in your home as a hot or neutral conductor because this incorrect usage presents a serious shock hazard. For more on grounding, see "Common problems with light fixtures," p. 123.

Safety First—and Last

Now that I've covered the basics of how the system works, let's talk safety. I joked earlier about people's fears of electrical work, but in reality, a little fear is a great thing. My fear of electricity helps me to maintain a healthy respect for the systems I work on, and your fear will help to keep you safe by alerting you to potential hazards.

The number-one safety rule I stress with my coworkers is something my high-school driving instructor once said: "If you don't know, don't go." Know your limitations. Unless you know that what you're doing is completely safe, don't

WORK SAFELY WITH ELECTRICITY

Follow these steps, in order, to minimize the risk of shock or electrocution.

1. IDENTIFY THE PROBLEM and the solution.

2. IDENTIFY THE CIRCUIT(S) you need to work on, and determine the means for disconnecting the circuit (breaker or fuse). If the circuits are not identified in the panel, you'll have to do some testing to find out which breaker or fuse controls which circuit. Even if they seem well labeled, it's still prudent to do some testing to verify.

3. DE-ENERGIZE THE CIRCUIT(S) by turning off the breaker or pulling the fuse.

4. VERIFY THE CORRECT CIRCUIT HAS BEEN SHUT OFF by checking the wiring and fixtures on that circuit with an electrical tester.

5. LOCK OUT THE PANEL to prevent anyone from energizing the circuit while you're working. You can simply tape the panel door shut and mark it with a warning.

6. COMPLETE YOUR WORK on the circuit.

7. DOUBLE-CHECK THAT THE WIRING IS PROPERLY SECURED to the device (switch, socket, or fixture) you're working on and that the ground wires are properly attached.

8. REPLACE ANY COVER PLATES removed during the work.

9. RE-ENERGIZE THE CIRCUIT and confirm operation.

HOW TO REPLACE AN OUTLET

1. PLUG IN A LAMP or use a tester to identify the proper circuit. (You might use nearby switches to determine if it's a switched outlet; see p. 120.) Turn off the power, and check to be sure using a testing device.

2. UNSCREW THE OUTLET and pull it out of the box. If you haven't already determined whether the outlet is switched, check the side tabs now (see p. 120).

3. ONCE YOU'VE ASSESSED THE SETUP of the outlet, remove the wires from the terminal screws and attach the new outlet in the same way. In a typical non-switched receptacle, the green (or bare) ground wire goes to the green grounding screw; the neutral (white) wire(s) goes to the silver terminal(s); and the hot (black) wire(s) goes to the gold terminal(s).

4. SECURE THE NEW OUTLET and replace the cover plate.

5. RE-ENERGIZE THE CIRCUIT, and check your work.

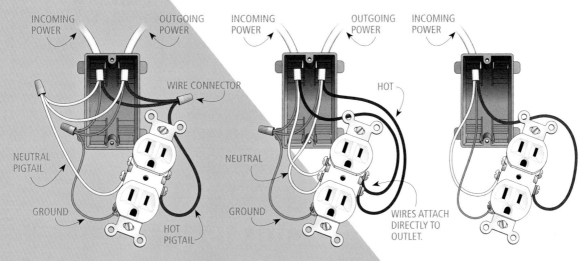

SPLICING WIRES WITH PIGTAILS (short wires) to the outlet ensures continuous current downstream, even if the outlet fails.

ATTACHING HOT AND NEUTRAL WIRES directly to the outlet's terminals is quicker and results in a less crowded box, but if the outlet fails, it can interrupt power downstream.

AT THE END OF A CIRCUIT, there is only one cable coming into the box, and all wires are connected directly to the outlet (no pigtails).

do it. That means turning off the power when you're working on a circuit. It's not worth the risk of getting shocked or electrocuted, even if you have to shut down the whole house to be sure the wires you're handling are off.

I always shudder when I hear people say, "It's OK—it's only 120 volts" when referring to the possibility of electric shock. Let me be perfectly clear: 120v household current can and will kill you if you don't protect yourself. The side-bar on the facing page outlines the safe work procedure I use. I advise you to use it, too.

Another crucial safety rule is to follow any and all directions provided with the devices or equipment you're working on. Even the most basic electrical devices come with directions, so take the time to read through them before you start, and again after you're done to make sure you didn't miss anything. When I come across a problem in someone else's wiring, 99% of the time it's because someone didn't follow simple directions.

1. Replace an Outlet

Outlets (aka receptacles or sockets) are easily the most abused portion of a home's electrical system—constantly pushed, pulled, wiggled, and jiggled. If you suspect an outlet is bad, plug in a lamp and wiggle the plug around a little. If the light flickers, you've found the problem. After you've turned off the power and unscrewed the faulty outlet from the box, you're likely to see one of three configurations, depending on whether the outlet is in the middle or at the end of a circuit, and whether it's wired so that power runs both through and past it (using pigtails; left drawing, p. 119) or just through it (center drawing, p. 119).

Swap switched outlets

Switched outlets are just that—outlets controlled by a switch so that you can plug in a lamp and use a switch to turn it on and off.

Most switched outlets have a constant power source on one half of the outlet and a switched power source on the other. The easiest way to tell is if you have two different-color hot wires attached to the same outlet, and the little metal tab between the hot (gold) screws has been removed, enabling each outlet to operate independently. The drawing below shows one arrangement in which the switch controls only the bottom half of the split-tab outlet. The top half of the split-tab outlet and the next outlet in the circuit have constant power.

When replacing a switched outlet, you need to remove the tab between the hot terminals on the new outlet so that they can operate independently. Be sure to attach the hot wires as they were on the old device so that the same half remains switched.

2. Replace a Single-Pole Switch

The next time you're at the hardware store grumbling about having to replace an unresponsive light switch, think about this: How much quality do you expect from a piece of equipment that costs less than a buck? The fact is that switches fail for lots of reasons besides product quality, including poor connections by the electrician, expansion and contraction of metal parts over time, and rough handling.

HOW TO SWAP SWITCHED OUTLETS

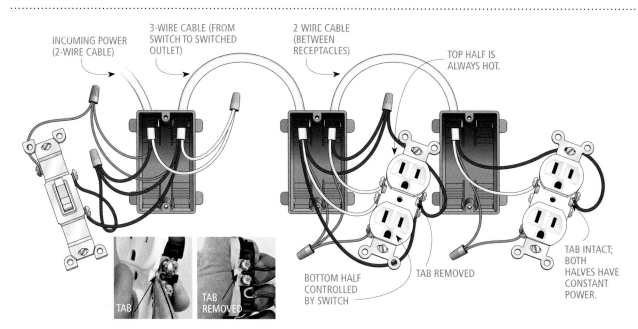

INCOMING POWER (2-WIRE CABLE)

3-WIRE CABLE (FROM SWITCH TO SWITCHED OUTLET)

2 WIRE CABLE (BETWEEN RECEPTACLES)

TOP HALF IS ALWAYS HOT.

TAB

TAB REMOVED

BOTTOM HALF CONTROLLED BY SWITCH

TAB REMOVED

TAB INTACT; BOTH HALVES HAVE CONSTANT POWER.

HOW TO REPLACE A SINGLE-POLE SWITCH

1. TURN OFF THE BREAKER or pull the fuse supplying power to the box containing the switch. If the box contains multiple switches, be aware that each switch may be on a different circuit, and make sure everything is off by checking the operation of each switch and using a testing device.

2. REMOVE THE COVER PLATE with a ³/₁₆-in. flat-blade screwdriver.

3. UNSCREW THE SWITCH FROM THE BOX, and pull it out to access the terminal screws. The neutrals will be connected together in the back of the box; leave them alone. Disconnect the two hot leads from the switch's terminals (usually on the right side). Bare or green ground wires coming into the box will also connect to the box (if it is metal) and/or the switch itself. If the ground wire is attached to the switch, disconnect it.

4. MAKE SURE THE NEW SWITCH IS ORIENTED CORRECTLY (the printed word "OFF" should be on top of the switch) before attaching the wires. Attach the ground wire to the green terminal and the black wires to the hot terminals. (The switch will operate regardless of which hot wire goes to which hot terminal, but I always route the incoming power wire to the bottom and the outgoing power to the top.)

5. REPLACE THE COVER PLATE, and restore power to the circuit. Test the switch for proper operation.

TYPICAL SINGLE-POLE SWITCH

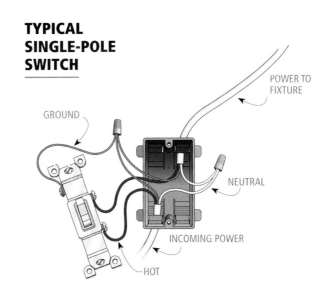

GROUND

POWER TO FIXTURE

NEUTRAL

INCOMING POWER

HOT

SWITCH LOOP

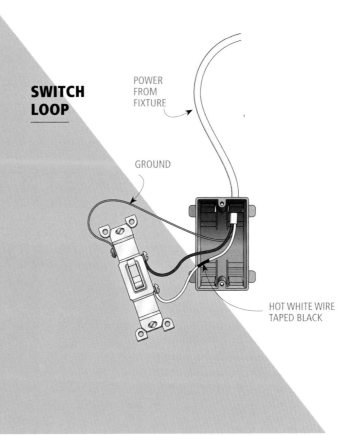

POWER FROM FIXTURE

GROUND

HOT WHITE WIRE TAPED BLACK

HOW TO REPLACE A THREE-WAY SWITCH

1. TURN OFF POWER TO ALL THE BOXES CONTAINING THE SWITCHES. Three-way switches can be tougher to replace than single-pole switches because there are at least two boxes involved, and you need to make sure the power is off to all the switches in each box. Verify everything is off by using a testing device.

2. REMOVE THE COVER PLATE, typically with a ³⁄₁₆-in. flat-blade screwdriver.

3. UNSCREW THE SWITCH FROM THE BOX, and pull it out to access the terminal screws. Make a note of which wire is attached to the common terminal and mark it. The common carries power either in to the switch or out to the fixture (drawing, right). The travelers' connections don't really need to be distinguished from one another as long as you know which two wires they are. Taping the two travelers together and leaving the common loose is another way to keep from getting confused.

4. REMOVE THE WIRES FROM THE SCREW TERMINALS ON THE SWITCH, and replace it with the new switch. Reattach the ground wire to the green ground screw; make sure the traveler wires go to the traveler terminals, and the common wire goes to the common terminal. See the drawings at right for additional wiring details that apply to your specific situation.

5. REPLACE THE COVER PLATE, and restore power to the circuit. Test the switch for proper operation.

LIGHT IN MIDDLE

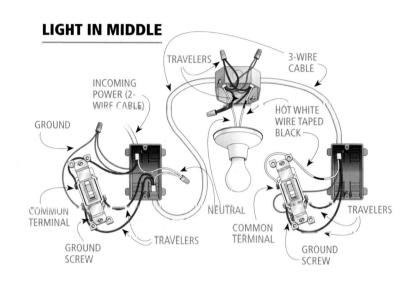

LIGHT FIRST

LIGHT AT END

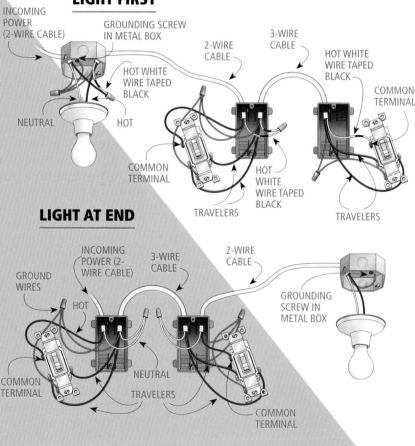

A single-pole switch is simply a switch that works alone to turn a fixture on and off. It is generally wired in one of two ways: one in which power comes to the switch first; and another, called a switch loop (bottom drawing, p. 121), in which power comes into the fixture and then is routed to the switch. Although the wires might look a bit different, they hook up to the switch the same way.

If you open a switch box and see only one cable coming in, it's probably a switch loop. Because there is only one cable in a switch loop, the white "neutral" functions as a "hot" to complete the circuit. To designate this, the white wire must be marked with black tape or marker. This marked wire is attached to one of the screw terminals just as a black "hot" would be (bottom drawing, p.121).

3. Replace a Three-Way Switch

Whereas a single-pole switch is one switch that controls one fixture, a three-way switch is used when two switches control the same fixture. It may seem counterintuitive to call them "three-way" because they work in pairs. The name refers to their operation, so don't let it confuse you. The wiring will do that.

One reason three-way switches confuse people is because they are wired differently depending on the relative position of the fixture(s) and the switches. But there are some common denominators. Three-way switches have three terminal screws: Two are typically brass-colored, and one is usually black or dark and labeled "common." The coloring and labeling are important because the wiring must be connected in a specific way for the switches to operate properly. The common on one switch is the "in" side of the setup from the power source, and the common on the other switch is the "out" to power the light. Two other wires, called travelers, run between the switches. Power on the travelers alternates depending on whether the switches they're connected to are off or on. If the sequence completes the circuit, the light is on. If not, it's off.

On the facing page are three typical setups you'll find when replacing a three-way switch. All things considered, the key to a simple three-way switch (pun intended) is to distinguish correctly the hot (common) wire from the travelers and to route all three to the correct terminals. The best way to do this is to identify and mark the wires carefully before disconnecting the old switch.

4. Replace a Light Fixture

Installing a new light fixture is about as straightforward a process as you will encounter when working on your electrical system. Perhaps because it's such a seemingly easy task, even the most electrically gun-shy folks I know will readily change out a light fixture. Perhaps that's also why, in the course of my remodeling work, most of the light fixtures I'm asked to change out are incorrectly installed (see "Common problems," below). Considering that most light fixtures are conductive (metal) and a part of the system that you will have routine contact with (changing bulbs, dusting, etc.), proper installation, including grounding, is a must. If yours is an older, ungrounded system, be sure to use an approved replacement or consult a professional.

Common problems with light fixtures

The biggest mistake I find with light fixtures is that they aren't installed in a box: I remove the light, and there's nothing behind it but a hole in the wall with a wire dangling out. All electrical connections within the confines of your home should be inside an electrical box approved for that use. Boxes not only provide a means to mount fixtures and wiring securely, but they also shield framing and other combustible materials in the event of a failed connection.

The second most common problem I uncover is that most light fixtures are not grounded. I can't count the number of light fixtures I've removed, only to have the ground wire come leaping out at me. I can only speculate that a lack of understanding is what makes this such a common problem.

So, to reiterate: Make sure that all fixtures are mounted in a box. Also, make sure that the fixture's grounding wire, if it has one, is securely fastened to the circuit's ground wire and to the screw on the fixture box, if it is a metal one. If yours is an older, ungrounded system (without a ground wire), use a replacement approved for ungrounded systems, or consult an electrician about installing a ground wire or adding GFCI (ground-fault circuit interrupter) protection to the circuit.

Brian Walo is an electrician in Mount Pleasant, S.C. Photos by Michael Litchfield. Drawings by Trevor Johnston.

HOW TO REPLACE A LIGHT FIXTURE

1. ALWAYS SHUT DOWN POWER TO THE CIRCUIT THE LIGHT IS ON instead of relying on the switch to determine that the power is off. With the numerous ways that wiring and switches can be configured, such as a switch loop, it's possible to have the switch in the off position and still have power in the fixture box.

2. REMOVE THE OLD LIGHT, marking which wires attach to which colored leads on the old fixture. Install a fixture box if one does not exist. Your local home center carries a variety of "old work" box options (seemingly counter-intuitive because it's a new fixture, but you're installing it into an existing or "old work" application).

3. INSTALL THE MOUNTING BRACKET FOR THE NEW LIGHT FIXTURE ON THE BOX, making sure it's securely fastened and the screw studs that support it are level so that it won't hang crookedly. After the bracket is installed, hold the fixture up to it and adjust the depth of the mounting-screw studs so that they allow for a tight fit of the fixture to the wall.

4. CONNECT THE FIXTURE'S WIRE LEADS TO THE APPROPRIATE LEADS IN THE BOX. The fixture's ground lead (if it has one) should be attached to the grounding wire and/or to the green-colored grounding screw on the box (if it is a metal one). Then connect the neutral (white) fixture lead to the neutral cable wire, and connect the black fixture lead to the hot cable wire.

5. ATTACH THE LIGHT FIXTURE SECURELY, re-energize the circuit, and check your work.

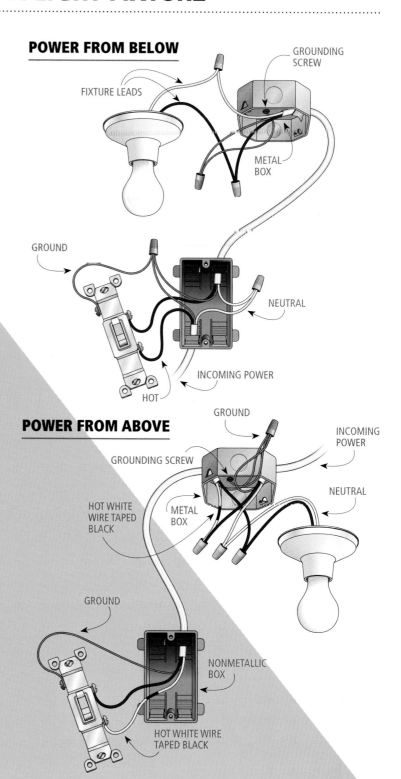

POWER FROM BELOW

GROUNDING SCREW

FIXTURE LEADS

METAL BOX

GROUND

NEUTRAL

INCOMING POWER

HOT

POWER FROM ABOVE

GROUND

INCOMING POWER

GROUNDING SCREW

HOT WHITE WIRE TAPED BLACK

METAL BOX

NEUTRAL

GROUND

NONMETALLIC BOX

HOT WHITE WIRE TAPED BLACK

Retrofitting a Ceiling Fan

BY CLIFFORD A. POPEJOY ▦ A ceiling fan is a great way to improve your comfort at home, and one of the most common retrofit projects is one that replaces an existing ceiling light with a fan that includes a light. Ceiling fans are easier than ever to assemble and install; in fact, I recently walked a friend through the process in an afternoon. Easy or not, there are a couple of important safety issues to keep in mind: avoiding electrical shock and getting the fan solidly attached to the ceiling framing.

Before you do anything, find out if the circuit has the capacity to run the new fixture. Most fan/light fixtures use two to three times more power than a standard light fixture. If the circuit was close to capacity before, you don't want to overload it.

Map out the circuit to determine what's on it. The easiest way is to turn off that particular circuit breaker and see what else no longer works. Add up the wattage of the lights and appliances that are fed by the circuit; be sure to include things that may not be used all the time, such as space heaters. If the total wattage is more than 1800w for a 15-amp circuit or more than 2400w for a 20-amp circuit, the circuit definitely is overloaded. Although not required by code, it's advisable to keep the load below 80% of those figures.

In the interest of proportion and efficiency, you have to match the fan size to the room. The chart below provides the basic guidelines; choose the next largest size if the fan is to be installed in a room with a high ceiling.

ROOM SIZE (SQ. FT.)	OVERALL BLADE DIAMETER (IN.)
100	36
144	42
225	44–48
400	52–54
500	56–60

Remove the Old Box, and Check the Existing Wires

Just shutting off the existing light at the wall switch doesn't guarantee that power is off in the ceiling box (sidebar, p. 129). The ceiling light's circuit should be turned off at the service panel. Use a voltage tester to confirm that the fixture and all the wires in the box are de-energized, and make sure they'll stay that way while you're working on them.

Now take a close look at the cables coming into the box; take notes on how they're connected. Sometimes it's helpful to label the wires with masking tape and a felt-tip pen. If the old ceiling box is a ½-in.-deep pancake-style box, removing it is usually just a matter of pulling some nails or a couple of screws. For a side-nailed box, I've found that the best removal tool to use is a hacksaw blade in a holder, or a reciprocating saw outfitted with a thin, short blade to cut the nails. Be careful that you don't chew up the wiring as you cut.

Installing a ceiling fan is a straightforward job

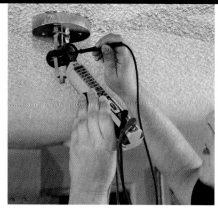

1 **MAKE SURE THE OLD FIXTURE IS DEAD.** After cutting power at the service panel, use a contact voltage tester to test the wires in the fixture box. Cover all but the end of the probe with electrical tape, which reduces the chance of shorting the probe to the fixture's shell if the power is not off.

2 **INSTALL THE HANGER.** After removing the old box, install the new. In this case, we used a fan-rated hanger bar and outlet box. The hanger bar is inserted first, squared up to the joists, and centered in the hole. The bar then is twisted clockwise, which pushes the barbed ends into the joists.

3 **INSERT THE NEW BOX.** Remove a knockout and insert a plastic cable clamp before attaching the box to the hanger bar. Slip the cables into the cable clamps as you slide the box into the hole. CONTINUED ON PAGE 128 ▶

USE A FAN-RATED BOX

Before installing a ceiling fan, electrical code requires that you use a fan-rated outlet box that will support the extra weight and the motion associated with a fan. A fan-rated box will be labeled as such inside and typically can support up to 70 lb.

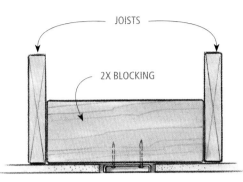

JOISTS

2X BLOCKING

LOW PROFILE

A ½-in.-deep pancake box is meant to be screwed to a joist or block. It's used if only one cable is coming into the box.

DEEPER PROFILE

A 2¼-in.-deep box can be attached to blocking between joists and is roomy enough to handle more than one cable. It is also available in a saddle-mount configuration.

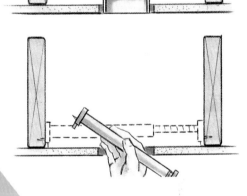

NO BLOCKING, NO PROBLEM

Paired with a deep box, this hanger is meant to span between two joists and takes the place of wooden blocking.

After removing the box, check the wires. If the insulation on the wires is old and deteriorated, use electrical tape or heat-shrink tubing (available in most electronics-supply stores) to insulate them. If the insulation is too cracked and you have access from above, cut back the old wires, install a splice (or junction) box, and run new cables to the fan-box location. If the wiring is armored (BX) cable, make sure the metal jacket is in good condition; if it's rusty or corroded, install a junction box and run new cable.

Finish Up with Solid Support and Elementary Wiring

During retrofits, the most common mistake is not to upgrade the outlet box. Use a fan-rated outlet box (sidebar, above) that's secured to solid blocking or framing. Also, when assembling the fan, be sure to use the rubber isolation pads included with it; they're meant to reduce wobbling and to stop fan noise from telegraphing to the ceiling.

AN EXTENSION KEEPS THE FAN AT THE RIGHT HEIGHT.
A fan is most efficient when its blades are 7 ft. to
9 ft. from the floor. For higher or sloped ceilings, fans
typically are suspended from extension rods, available
in varying lengths from manufacturers.

Follow the manufacturers' instructions on the wiring. Typically, the colors of the wires in the ceiling box are matched with the fixture wires: green or bare copper ground to fixture green, white to white fixture, and black to black fixture.

For a fan with a light, there are two supply wires in the fixture, one for the fan power and one for the light power (often black and blue, or black and black with a blue stripe). If you're controlling the light and the fan with one wall switch, connect both of them to the supply wire (usually black) in the ceiling box.

If there are two wall switches, there will be a three-conductor-with-ground cable (12-3 wg) from the switch box to the ceiling box. I use the black conductor to control the light and the red to operate the fan. By convention, the switch for the light should be the one located closest to the door.

The light-fixture part of the fan is installed after the fan is hung. Some fan models have a factory-installed modular connector for the light fixture. Remove the cover at the

Installing a ceiling fan, continued

4 **CLEAN WIRES FOR A BETTER CONNECTION.**
Use the manufacturer's locknuts to attach the box, then clean the exposed wire ends with a nylon scrubby and make the splices as needed. Here, we used a UL-listed pressure connector because the wires were short and there was no practical way to splice in longer cables.

5 **SAVE YOURSELF A HEADACHE.** Once you've identified all the parts, thread the wires through as you assemble the fan motor, canopy trim ring, canopy, and base. Make sure the parts are assembled in the right order now, rather than later. Don't attach the blades until the fan body is in place.

bottom of the fan housing, plug in the light fixture, and fasten the fixture to the fan housing.

On other fan models, the light-fixture wires connect to the corresponding supply wires with twist-on wire connectors. I usually toss those and use the type that have wire springs inside; they make for a better connection.

Some ceiling-fan models have a remote-control unit that fits into a switch box so that no wires are needed between the wall switch and the fan. There must be power at the fan and at the switch, but sometimes, it's a lot easier to get power at those two locations and not have to run a switching cable between them.

The job isn't complete until you've checked the fan to make sure it's balanced. Run the fan at the highest speed; if it shakes or wobbles, check all the mounting hardware, starting with the ceiling box. Are all the screws, washers, and spacers in place and tight? Then examine the fan blades and arms, and replace any that are bent or warped.

Clifford A. Popejoy is a licensed electrical contractor in Sacramento, Calif. Photos by the author, except for the top photo on the facing page.

BE SURE THE POWER IS OFF

In older houses, alternative wiring schemes might literally shock an otherwise careful electrician. For instance, there may be power in the ceiling box even after the light is turned off at the wall switch. In one common scenario, power goes to the ceiling box and a switch loop is dropped to the switch. Or the box is used as a junction box, either for the light circuit or for the light and a different circuit.

A third possibility is that the wiring is just messed up; for instance, the hot and neutral wires may be reversed. Be sure to test the wiring with a good voltage tester (see "Working Safely Around Electricity," pp. 114–116). Also, use a ground reference—the grounded conductor socket of an extension cord that's plugged into a grounded outlet known to be good—with your voltage tester to check the polarity of wires, especially old ones that may not be color-coded.

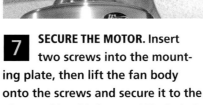

6 **HANG THE MOTOR.** After attaching the base or hanging bracket to the fan box with 10/24 or #12 screws, hang the fan body from the hook on the base, and splice the wires together with heavy-duty wire nuts.

7 **SECURE THE MOTOR.** Insert two screws into the mounting plate, then lift the fan body onto the screws and secure it to the plate. Add a third screw if included by the manufacturer, then slide the upper canopy in place.

8 **ATTACH THE LIGHTS.** This model included a light fixture, which attached to the underside of the fan body. The wiring connections usually are made with a snap fitting, and then the fixture is screwed to the fan body.

STANLEY

PLUMBING REPAIRS

A PLUMBING TOOL KIT

BY DAVID SCHIFF

1. Flanged plunger for unclogging a toilet

2. Toilet auger for unclogging a toilet

3. Drainpipe auger for unclogging a sink

4. Slip-joint pliers with two positions for grasping and turning

5. Phillips-head screwdrivers for most of the screws you'll encounter

6. Thin-blade flathead screwdrivers for lifting the decorative caps on faucet handles

7. Adjustable pliers for loosening tight hand nuts and installing a ball cartridge

8. Silicone for under gaskets if the top of the sink is pitted

9. Allen wrenches for removing the handles from single-handled faucets and replacing the seat for brass cartridges

10. Nailset for fishing out faucet valve seals and springs

11. Snips for cutting the collar off a new flush valve and cutting refill tube to length

12. Small adjustable wrench for water-supply connections and other nuts

13. Basin wrench for hard-to-reach nuts between the sink and the wall (usually needed only for replacing faucets on deep kitchen sinks)

David Schiff is an editorial project manager, writer, and editor with extensive experience in the areas of home improvement, construction, and woodworking. Photos by Jeffrey Goulding, photo-synthesis.co, except for the tool bucket photo.

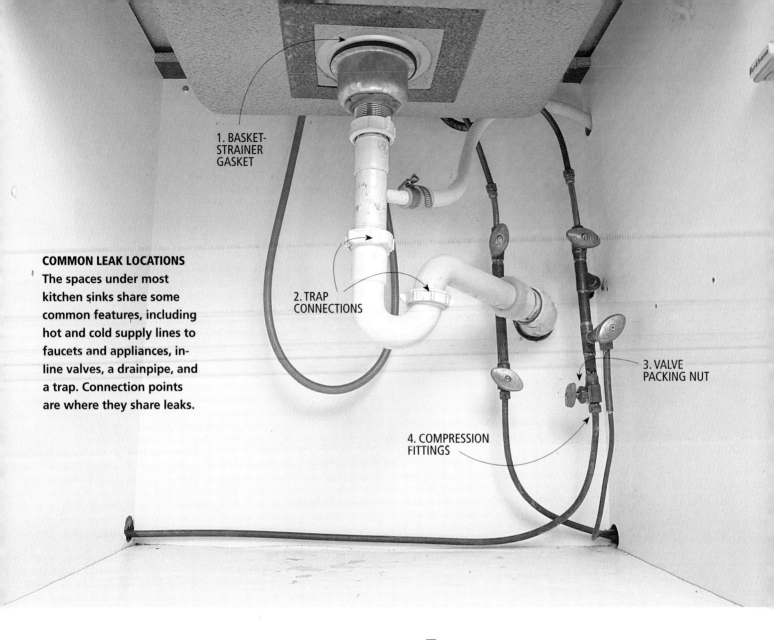

COMMON LEAK LOCATIONS
The spaces under most kitchen sinks share some common features, including hot and cold supply lines to faucets and appliances, in-line valves, a drainpipe, and a trap. Connection points are where they share leaks.

1. BASKET-STRAINER GASKET

2. TRAP CONNECTIONS

3. VALVE PACKING NUT

4. COMPRESSION FITTINGS

4 Easy-to-Fix Kitchen-Sink Leaks

BY TOM TIMAN   As a professional plumber, I go on lots of repair calls for leaking sinks. In about half of those cases, it takes me all of five minutes to remedy the problem.

Of course, then there's the next problem: the customer's anger over shelling out $125 for a five-minute service call. The truth is, when you call a plumber, you get a trained, licensed professional along with a truck stocked with hundreds of parts. Most of the time, that's way more firepower than anyone needs when they find a puddle under the kitchen sink.

Undersink leaks can be a hassle, but a little detective work along with a few tools and an understanding of how common plumbing fittings work will have your cabinet floor dry in no time. There are four primary locations where kitchen-sink pipes tend to leak; I'll go through identifying and fixing them step-by-step. I'll also point out a number of less common leaks (sidebar, p. 135) that involve a little more work, but most are still doable without calling a pro.

Before you can fix a leak, you have to find the source. A wet or dripping pipe is pretty obvious, although pinpointing the source on that pipe might be tricky; what looks like a leaking trap could be a loose gasket at the basket strainer. A good way to confirm what's leaking is to experiment with turning on the water (which will reveal a supply-line leak), running it down the drain (for a trap leak), or filling the sink (for a basket-strainer leak). In all these cases, a mechanical joint—where two parts come together—has failed or loosened. Cracks or pinholes in pipes or joints do occur, but they're not all that common.

There's no need to shut off the water for any of these repairs. In fact, keeping it on lets you know when you've stemmed the flow. But with that in mind, don't attempt any plumbing repairs without first locating the main shut-off for your house. In fact, even if they never put their head under a sink, every person in the household should know where and how to shut off the water. It's a simple precaution that too few people think about—until a valve gives way and there's water pouring all over the floor.

1. Basket-strainer gasket

You'll know you have a leaking basket strainer if the leak occurs only when there's standing water in the sink. The most common cause of this leak is a basket-strainer gasket (the black rubber ring that seals the connection between the sink and the drainpipe) that is no longer fully compressed.

BASKET-STRAINER GASKET

BASKET STRAINER

LOCKNUT

DRAIN TAILPIECE EXTENSION

TO COMPRESS THE GASKET, you'll need to tighten the locknut that holds the strainer to the sink. This nut is located either right under the gasket or under the basket (as shown here).

GET A GRIP. Use a large pair of pliers to get a good grip on the nut. Hold the drainpipe to prevent twisting, and tighten the nut. Occasionally, the tightening might force some plumber's putty from behind the ring inside the sink; just wipe it away.

2. Trap connections

Beneath every sink drain is a trap, a looped section of pipe. Water resting in the trap blocks noxious sewer gases from entering the home. The section of pipe creating the loop (called a P-trap) is attached to the tailpiece extension on one end and to the waste pipe (J-bend) on the other with slip nuts. If there's leakage here, it usually means that one of the slip nuts has been knocked loose and that the connection beneath it is leaking.

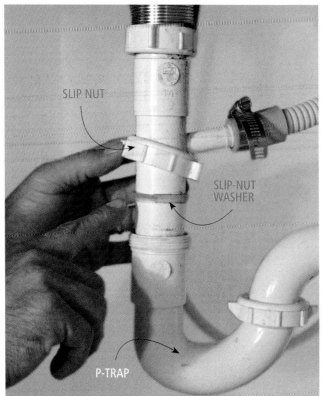

SLIP NUT

SLIP-NUT WASHER

P-TRAP

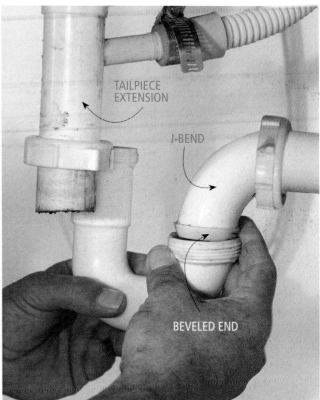

TAILPIECE EXTENSION

J-BEND

BEVELED END

REPLACE THE WASHER. If there's a leak where the trap meets the tailpiece extension, the culprit might be a cracked slip-nut washer. If so, replace it. Seat the washer firmly in the end of the P-trap before hand-tightening the slip nut over it. Be sure not to cross-thread the nut, and be sure to position the connection so that the J-bend pipe slopes down slightly toward the wall.

TO ELIMINATE LEAKS BETWEEN THE P-TRAP AND J-BEND, loosen the slip nut, and reseat the J-bend's bevel firmly in the trap. Hand-tighten the slip nut over the joint.

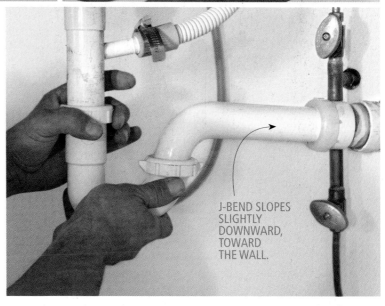

J-BEND SLOPES SLIGHTLY DOWNWARD, TOWARD THE WALL.

3. Valve packing nut

Another common leak involves a loose packing nut on a shutoff valve. Simply tightening this nut usually does the trick.

THE PACKING NUT is located behind the valve handle (shown here from the side).

TIGHTEN THE NUT. Hold the supply pipe firmly with one hand (for leverage and to keep from bending the pipe), and tighten the nut clockwise as snug as you can.

STILL LEAKING?

The four situations discussed in this article account for about half of the under-sink leaks I'm called to fix. Here are some other problems you might encounter.

LEAKING LAVATORY (FAUCET) SUPPLY CONNECTION

Occasionally, a leak will form where the supply pipe attaches to the faucet control. Fixing it depends on the faucet manufacturer and model; each one is different. Your best defense is always to save the installation booklet when you install a new faucet. In it, you'll find helpful diagrams and information on parts that will help you fix whatever problem arises. Don't have the booklet? There's a good chance you'll find it on the manufacturer's website.

LOOSE AUXILIARY APPLIANCE HOSES

As things are jostled underneath the sink, hoses that connect to dishwashers, ice makers, coffeemakers, and the like can come loose. They are usually connected with hose clamps. You can tighten the clamp with a screwdriver, or add another clamp for a more secure seal.

SEEPAGE AROUND SINK RIM

If you let dishes drip-dry on the counter, you might notice water seeping around the rim of a drop-in sink. Cure this by running a thin bead of clear tub-and-tile caulk where the sink meets the countertop. Smooth the line with your finger, and remove the excess with a wet paper towel, wiping in short strokes away from the rim.

PINHOLES IN COPPER PIPES

If copper pipes are leaking, but not at a mechanical joint, there might be a pinhole in the pipe itself. Pinholes usually require cutting out the leaking section and soldering a new section in its place. Soldering copper plumbing can be tricky; the line needs to be completely dry to get a durable seal. Unless you're handy with a blowtorch and experienced at this type of work, this is one job you might leave for the $125-an-hour guy.

4. Compression fittings

Kitchen-sink supply lines generally come equipped with one or more shutoff valves. One source of leaks—especially if the lines are routinely jostled by buckets, bottles, and other supplies kept under a sink—is the compression fitting that typically connects one end of the shutoff valve to the line. These fittings consist of a nut that tightens over a brass ferrule or compression ring, squeezing it and creating a watertight seal. If the nut is knocked loose, the joint can leak.

Tom Timan is a licensed plumber in Connecticut.

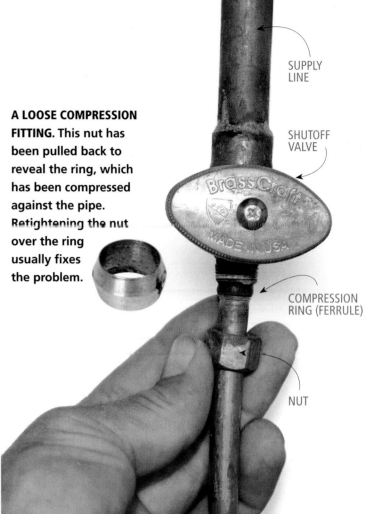

A LOOSE COMPRESSION FITTING. This nut has been pulled back to reveal the ring, which has been compressed against the pipe. Retightening the nut over the ring usually fixes the problem.

SUPPLY LINE

SHUTOFF VALVE

COMPRESSION RING (FERRULE)

NUT

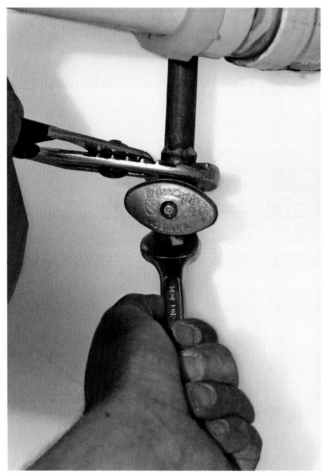

KEEP THINGS IN LINE. Grip the valve with channel-lock pliers to prevent the pipe from twisting while you tighten the nut with a ⅝-in. open-end wrench. Make the nut as tight as you can.

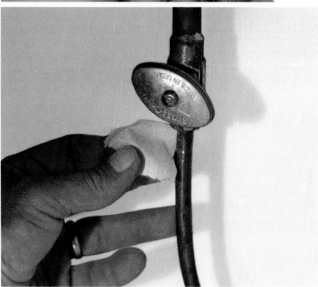

CHECK YOUR WORK. After tightening the nut, dry the valve completely, and touch it lightly with a piece of paper (toilet tissue works best) to confirm the seal.

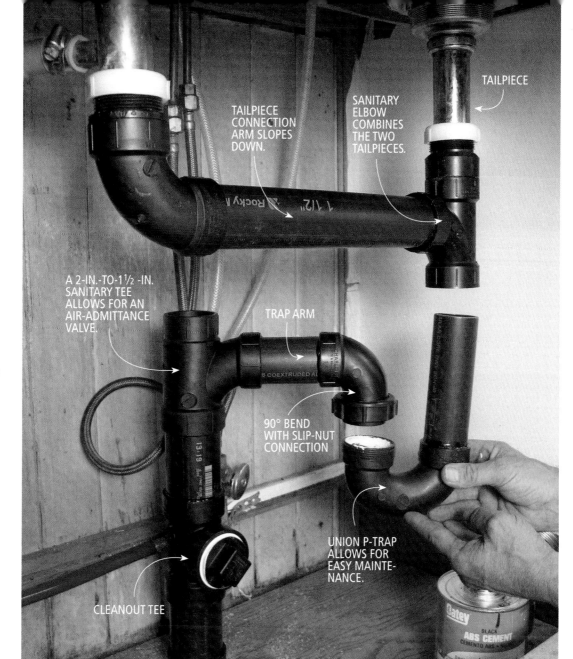

TAILPIECE

TAILPIECE CONNECTION ARM SLOPES DOWN.

SANITARY ELBOW COMBINES THE TWO TAILPIECES.

A 2-IN.-TO-1½-IN. SANITARY TEE ALLOWS FOR AN AIR-ADMITTANCE VALVE.

TRAP ARM

90° BEND WITH SLIP-NUT CONNECTION

UNION P-TRAP ALLOWS FOR EASY MAINTE-NANCE.

CLEANOUT TEE

UNDERSINK PLUMB-ING AT A GLANCE. An undersink P-trap is a vulnerable piece of plumbing. Plumbed wrong, it can be a constant headache. Plumbed right, you might never have to think about it again.

Replacing a Sink Trap

BY BRUCE NORMAN ▪ Sink traps may need replacement for a few different reasons. Because the undersink area is regularly used as storage, the exposed trap assembly is bumped and jostled and can become damaged.

Also, the trap assembly might not have been installed correctly, and its horizontal runs could be insufficiently pitched and not drain well. Finally, the trap could be an outdated configuration, such as an S-trap, which has been eliminated under most code jurisdictions. While some traps can be taken apart and cleaned to restore proper flow, I recommend rebuilding the entire trap assembly.

The two materials most often used for sink plumbing are PVC and ABS (acrylonitrile butadiene styrene). For the repair featured here, I used ABS because the joints are bonded with one-part glue as opposed to the two-part glue needed for PVC. I use glued joints wherever possible but incorporate threaded unions at the trap and tailpieces for serviceability. For this sink, I added a cleanout below the trap assembly, which is required by code. Then I added the sanitary tee to allow for venting.

Originally, there was no vent to this old S-trap system, which is common for old plumbing. Most codes require the vent to be restored to allow liquid to drain quickly. In this case, I installed an air-admittance valve (AAV). Check with your local building department for any restrictions if you choose to use an AAV.

Bruce Norman lives with his wife, Hildi, in Portland, Ore. Drawing by Toby Welles/WowHouse.

Combine the tailpieces, then build from the bottom up

1 CONNECT THE TAILPIECES. Use a 90° bend and a sanitary tee with slip-nut connections to draw the drain water into one tailpiece. The connection arm should slope down by ¼ in. per ft. Provide a stub for the dishwasher drain in the tailpiece, if needed.

2 MEASURE TO CONNECT THE CLEANOUT. Hold the cleanout close to the floor but high enough to allow easy access to it. Measure between the hubs, and add ¾ in. for each flange. In this case, a 3¼-in. clear distance plus 1½ in. for the two flanges demands a 4-in. connector pipe.

Dry-fit the connections before gluing

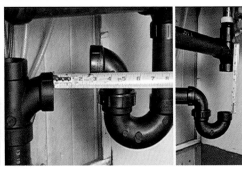

1 WORK YOUR WAY UP. Hold the 2-in.-to-1½-in. sanitary tee and the union P-trap in place. Measure the distance from the cleanout tee to the sanitary tee. Remember to add ¾ in. for each hub flange.

2 AIM THE T TOWARD THE TAILPIECE. Sight from behind the tailpiece to align the sanitary tee. There is some room for error, but try to get it as close as possible.

3 MEASURE FOR THE TRAP ARM. Dry-fit the P-trap with a scrap piece of pipe. Measure between the hub flanges, and add 1½ in. (¾ in. for each). Once the trap arm is cut, repeat the process to measure for the vertical tailpiece connection.

QUIET THE MONSTERS IN THE PIPES

Stories of monsters in drain lines originated with unvented plumbing. The simple act of dumping a big pot of spaghetti water down the drain can awaken the beast. As water drains, the pressure buildup causes a grumbled protest accompanied by an occasional clank in the pipes below. Once the flow gets going, though, suction takes hold, and the hot water is ingested through a plumbing system that probably has more turns in it than a giant-size Silly Straw. If you bend over and peer down the drain just as the slurping sound gets loudest, it will suddenly stop, and you'll be welcomed by a belch of raw sewer gas that has come through the now empty P-trap. Quelling the monster is an easy fix. For less than $30, you can buy an air-admittance valve (AAV) at your local plumbing-supply store.

John Ross, a former *Fine Homebuilding* editor, is a freelance writer, editor, photographer, and video producer.

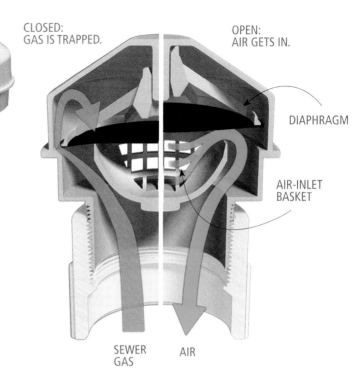

CLOSED: GAS IS TRAPPED.

OPEN: AIR GETS IN.

DIAPHRAGM

AIR-INLET BASKET

SEWER GAS

AIR

Glue everything but the threaded connections

1 LEVEL THE THREADED P-TRAP CONNECTION. Before the glue dries, level the threaded end of the union P-trap in both directions. This allows the rest of the connections to fit together squarely.

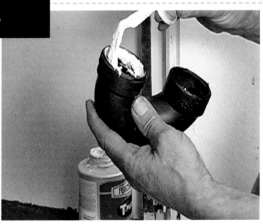

2 USE PIPE DOPE ON THE P-TRAP THREADS. When gluing the P-trap into place, use pipe dope on the threaded portion that connects to the union elbow. Dope ensures that this vulnerable spot won't leak over time.

Replacing a Garbage Disposal

BY ED CUNHA ▥ As a plumber, I get a lot of calls about garbage-disposal problems. I've seen an amazing variety of items take a disposal out of commission—everything from knickknacks to twist ties, bottle caps, and beef bones. But a disposal also can stop working for other reasons. The motor can overheat and seize, or an internal part can simply wear out or break.

When I arrive on the job, I have a strategy that tells me in a matter of minutes if the existing disposal can be fixed. If the troubleshooting tips don't work, there is a good chance your disposal is beyond repair. New disposals are relatively inexpensive and easy to install, so even if the old disposal is shot, it's not the end of the world (see "Install the new disposal," p. 142).

Because a disposal can mash fingers just as easily as it mashes food waste, I never work on this appliance without making sure the power is off. You might simply be able to unplug the disposal from a receptacle inside the cabinet. Otherwise, you'll need to flip a switch or a circuit breaker.

Ed Cunha is a plumber on Cape Cod, Mass. Drawing courtesy of InSinkErator.

RESET THE MOTOR. When the disposal's motor is overloaded, an internal circuit breaker can trip and shut down the unit. Pressing the red reset button on the underside of the disposal restores power, and the motor might be able to free itself.

SPIN THE GRINDING CHAMBER TO CLEAR THE JAM. With the power off, wedge a broom handle against the side of the grinding chamber, and use your hand as a pivot point. Alternatively, some units might accept a Jam-Buster™ Allen wrench that could free the jam.

Remove the old disposal

1 DISCONNECT THE DRAIN LINE. The drain outlet is near the middle of the disposal. On this unit, I could loosen the drain and disconnect the disposal by hand. Near the top, disconnect the dishwasher inlet as well.

2 REMOVE THE DISPOSAL WITH A TWIST. I like to sit on the floor and support the disposal with my foot. You don't have to be as flexible as you might think to do this. With both hands, rotate the disposal counterclockwise until the mounting assembly disconnects.

3 REMOVE THE MOUNTING ASSEMBLY. With a screwdriver, loosen the mounting screws and pry off the snap ring on the lower part of the assembly. Once that's removed, gently break the putty bond of the sink strainer, and remove the assembly from above.

A QUIETER GRIND

Garbage disposals can pulverize the scraps of food from a four-course meal, but they also can grind after-dinner conversation to a halt. The folks at InSinkErator® (www.insinkerator.com) have tuned their ears to this problem and are trying to improve the around-the-sink ambience. Their ¾-hp Premier model has more-than-adequate power but also incorporates sound-dampening features like a specially designed drain baffle, an insulated motor housing, and an antivibration motor mount. Available at home centers for around $200, it won't chew up the home-repair fund.

STRAINER

DRAIN BAFFLE

DISHWASHER INLET

ANTIVIBRATION MOTOR MOUNT

INSULATED MOTOR HOUSING

DRAIN LINE

Install the new disposal

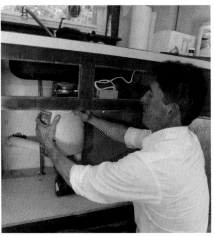

1 INSTALL THE STRAINER AND MOUNTING ASSEMBLY. Remove old putty from the lip of the drain. Apply new putty to the strainer, and press it in place. From below, slip on the paper gasket, the backup flange, and the mounting ring, in that order. Without pushing up on the assembly, install the snap ring and tighten the screws against the backup flange.

2 WIRE THE DISPOSAL FOR POWER. Whether direct-wiring the power source or installing an outlet plug, the operation is the same. On the bottom of the disposal, firmly secure the ground wire. Then connect like-color wires: white to white, black to black. Push the wires back into the housing and attach the cover plate.

3 HANG THE DISPOSAL ON THE MOUNTING ASSEMBLY. I use my foot to support the disposal the same way I did when I took it off. Align the mounting tabs with the mounting ring, and twist the mounting ring clockwise until it clicks into place. After the drain line is reconnected, fill the sink with water, and look at all the joints for possible leaks.

Installing a Toilet

BY MIKE LOMBARDI ■ Ask a group of plumbers the proper way to install a toilet, and the conversation can get heated quickly. There are two major points of controversy: where to mount the flange and whether you should caulk the bottom of the toilet to the floor.

When I install a toilet, I always make sure the closet flange is on top of the finished floor and anchored securely. This gives me the best chance for a sturdy, long-lasting, leak-free installation because the weight of the toilet and any occupant is transferred to the floor, not the connected piping.

Equally important, when the flange is on top of the finished floor, the outlet on the bottom of the toilet (the horn) is positioned so that it's below the top edge of the flange. This makes the wax seal last longer because the wax isn't being worn away by the constant flow of water. It also better protects the soft wax from the spiral-shaped hook at the end of toilet and drain snakes.

When connecting a toilet to the closet flange, I use plastic closet bolts. The bolts have chunky shoulders that help to hold them upright so that they're ready to accept the toilet as it's lowered into place. The bolts won't rust and will break if overtightened, a safeguard against cracking the toilet's base.

Caulking the bottom of the toilet to the floor is required by the International Plumbing Code and the International Residential Code.

Mike Lombardi is the owner of Lombardi Plumbing in Danbury, Conn.

1 **SECURE THE FLANGE.** Dry-fit the flange so that when the closet bolts are at the end of the mounting slots, they will be 12 in. from the wall behind the toilet. When fitting is done, glue the parts together. Screw the flange to the subfloor with zinc-coated screws, and install the closet bolts.

2 **DRY-FIT THE BOWL.** To identify installation problems early, always do a dry-fit. Because this bowl isn't quite level and has a slight rock, the author uses rubber-gasket material as a shim. Once he's satisfied, he removes the bowl and trims the rubber to fit around the flange.

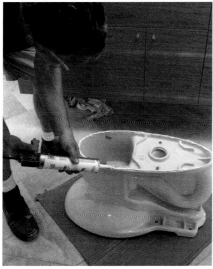

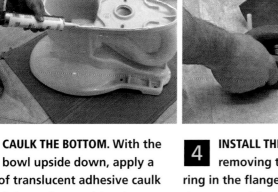

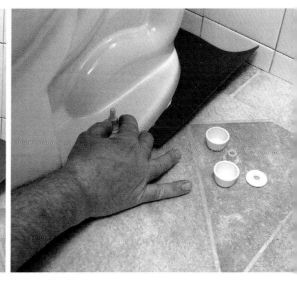

3 **CAULK THE BOTTOM.** With the bowl upside down, apply a bead of translucent adhesive caulk around the entire outside edge. This important sanitary measure is required by the IRC and the plumbing code.

4 **INSTALL THE WAX RING.** After removing the plug, place the ring in the flange. This ensures that the wax seal is centered over the toilet outlet. The author prefers the plastic-horned Hercules Johni-Ring®.

5 **FASTEN THE BOWL.** Carefully lower the bowl over the closet bolts. Lean on the bowl, compressing the wax seal until the bowl is in full contact with the floor. Then, with the cap bottoms in place, tighten the two bolts a little at a time.

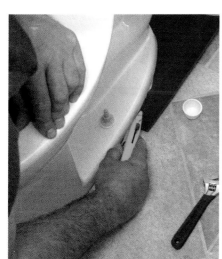

6 **TRIM THE SHIM.** Holding a utility knife so that the blade angles in, trim the rubber gasket flush with the bottom of the toilet. Use a fresh blade, and make the cut in several passes so that the blade doesn't slip and scratch the floor.

7 **INSTALL THE TANK GASKET.** In a conventional two-piece toilet, a soft rubber gasket seals the tank to the bowl. The brass bolts are tightened with a long socket provided by the toilet manufacturer. Go easy; overtightening can crack the tank.

CONTINUED ON PAGE 146 ▶

CONTINUED FROM PAGE 145

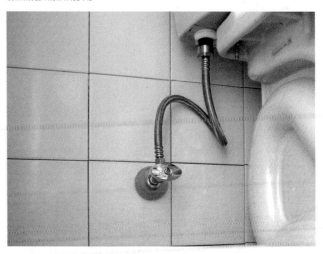

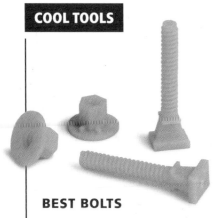

BEST BOLTS

Plastic closet bolts won't rust, and they'll break before they're tight enough to crack the toilet. Square shoulders keep the bolts upright in the flange.

SHIM STOCK

Rubber gasket makes an excellent shim for rocking bowls. This long-lasting material, available in the plumbing section of home centers, is impervious to water, is easy to cut, and molds to uneven surfaces.

SUPERIOR SEAL

The author likes translucent Phenoseal® for sealing the bottom of the bowl to the floor. The sealant prevents water from getting under the bowl.

8 **CONNECT THE SUPPLY.** The author likes to use braided supply lines with brass nuts at both ends. Choose one long enough to put a loop in the tubing. This puts less stress on the ends, which is where most leaks and breaks occur. Both ends have rubber washers, so the connections don't have to be tightened excessively.

9 **CAULK AGAIN.** Flush the toilet several times, inspecting the toilet and the basement for leaks. Once everything looks OK, apply another bead of caulk to seal the base to the floor, and smooth the joint with a moistened finger.